How May I Help You?

The publisher gratefully acknowledges the generous support of the Chairman's Circle of the University of California Press Foundation, whose members are:

Stephen A. & Melva Arditti

Elizabeth & David Birka-White

James & Carlin Naify

Ralph & Shirley Shapiro

Peter J. & Chinami S. Stern

How May I Help You?

*An Immigrant's Journey from
MBA to Minimum Wage*

Deepak Singh

UNIVERSITY OF CALIFORNIA PRESS

University of California Press, one of the most
distinguished university presses in the United
States, enriches lives around the world by
advancing scholarship in the humanities, social
sciences, and natural sciences. Its activities are
supported by the UC Press Foundation and by
philanthropic contributions from individuals and
institutions. For more information, visit www.
ucpress.edu.

University of California Press
Oakland, California

Library of Congress Cataloging-in-Publication Data

Names: Singh, Deepak, 1973- author.
Title: How may I help you? : an immigrant's journey from
    MBA to minimum wage / Deepak Singh.
Description: Oakland, California : University of California
    Press, [2017]
Identifiers: LCCN 2016030114| ISBN 9780520293304 (cloth :
    alk. paper) | ISBN 0520293304 (cloth : alk. paper) | ISBN
    9780520293311 (pbk. : alk. paper) | ISBN 0520293312 (pbk. :
    alk. paper) | ISBN 9780520966475 (ebook)
Subjects: LCSH: Foreign workers—United States. |
    Working poor—United States. | Immigrants—United
    States—Economic conditions. | United States—
    Economic conditions.
Classification: LCC HD8081.A5 S55 2016 |
    DDC 331.6/2092—dc23
LC record available at https://lccn.loc.gov/2016030114

Manufactured in the United States of America

26 25 24 23 22 21 20 19 18 17
10 9 8 7 6 5 4 3 2 1

For my parents, who worried for me, but never stopped me from finding my own path, and Holly, who traveled it with me, and Anushka, who joined us along the way

CONTENTS

FOREWORD

HOLLY DONAHUE SINGH

How May I Help You? takes on the issues of the working poor, immigration, and diversity in the United States through an intimate portrait of people living these realities, including the author himself. The story is not one of dire poverty or of illegal migration. Instead, it is an account about people living at the edge of hope and at the edge of making it, piecing together their lives around work, family, and other responsibilities, while finding ways to enjoy life. It's about a daily grind that's familiar to many people in the United States, yet the daily realities of which rarely capture national attention beyond debates about wages. As a new adult immigrant to the United States, Deepak Singh paid closer attention to his colleagues, his customers, and his environment than a native-born worker, someone who might learn the ropes and take the rest of the job for granted, would have. That perspective, along with his attention to storytelling, developed through writing for radio and other popular media, makes this a book that is deeply ethnographic and poignant, yet, at moments, also funny and lighthearted.

The United States that many Indians of Deepak's generation knew was *America* or even *Amrika,* a dreamland that, in contrast to India, was filled with rich people, clean air and water, and an unlimited supply of electricity. What Deepak found was something else. This combination of perspectives makes the book well suited to foster thoughtful discussion about how life looks to people engaged in service work and about the possibilities for structural and cultural transformation in the United States.

While every person's experiences are necessarily idiosyncratic, to a certain degree, Deepak's story highlights themes studied and debated by scholars and activists. For instance, Deepak's downward mobility in the workplace after his arrival underlines the difficulties many immigrants experience in finding a niche in a highly differentiated economy stratified between low-paid service work and highly compensated tech skills. Deepak was someone who didn't "fit" into either category easily. He had a master's degree in business, fluency in English, and legal permission to work. From India, he brought experience working for the British Broadcasting Corporation as a radio producer, as well as a long history of working with scholars from American and British universities and international professionals from organizations such as the World Health Organization and UNICEF. Still, after months of searching, he could land only a low-wage position. Other professionally trained immigrants, especially those with limited English skills, also find themselves faced with few options. Doctors become nurse's aides, lawyers become office workers, and teachers become tutors in an economic environment that is based on narrow credentials and is unforgiving of training outside the United States.

In a related vein, we glean from Deepak's observation the complex work life of his low-paid colleagues, struggling to make it as single mothers and minority employees and given little control over their work environments. Deepak's evolving relationship with the fellow employee he calls Ron, a middle-aged African American man trying to keep his job, his house, his health, and his current wife, is an especially moving example of how the conditions of work and social position affect workers' life trajectories. Workers in these low-prestige positions have few options when children get sick or transportation falls through. Both Ron and Jackie struggled to complete the managers' training program, which compelled them to take on extra responsibilities at the store and to drive themselves to meetings in a nearby town. Broken-down cars, sick children, and a lack of backup options for dealing with the inevitable ups and downs of daily life presented major barriers to the relative security of job and salary promised by a promotion to management. Unprotected by unions and often accruing little vacation or sick time, these service workers are on the front lines, and they are thrown away when they can't fulfill the exacting regulations around their positions.

Deepak also underscores how overt racism and a more subtle sense of unfamiliarity colors the work environment for immigrants. His "otherness" as a nonwhite employee possessing an ethnicity not clearly understood by most of his customers or colleagues led to confusion about his ethnicity and race. His customers didn't understand how he spoke or how to categorize him. However, his otherness and ambiguous identity also afforded him an opportunity to ask questions, to joke, and to makes mistakes that colleagues and customers might not have otherwise tolerated. Over time, Deepak and his colleagues learned from each other, smoothed the friction that emerged at times, and laughed together. Deepak's experiences, refracted through the lens of his knowledge of privilege and oppression, stemming from his upbringing in India, compel us to come to terms with our racial and ethnic insensitivity and ignorance in this storied land of "diversity" that is the contemporary United States.

As an anthropologist who was in training to conduct long-term ethnographic fieldwork in India during the time chronicled here, I am struck by how Deepak's particular social position in India and his disposition toward life help him draw readers along with him into his world of work as an outsider-insider in a low-wage position. Although the job had trappings of respectability, exemplified by the dress shirt and pants he ironed to wear to work each day and the lure of being promoted into management, it also came with no easy escape into middle-class life in the United States or back to the world of relative privilege he had come from in India. As the author's significant other and partner in his journey to the United States, I am the one, in some sense, who both enabled his journey and prevented his escape back to the comforts of his old life in India. I read this story with both pride and pain.

I come from a working-class family and did service work as a convenience store employee, a waitress, and a housecleaner before graduate school. I was sometimes a poor informant and supporter to Deepak because service work was so routine and normal to me and to others in my family. At other times, I failed because the range of people Deepak encountered at work exceeded the bounds of my social world, then comprised by white working-class rural western Pennsylvania, urban India, and academia. Although we had known each other for years in India, shared knowledge of both Hindi and English, and were in constant contact by email, letters, and phone, I was just twenty-five, sharing a house with other graduate students, and finishing a master's degree on the way to a doctorate when he arrived. We struggled to build our life together in Virginia. As I spent time with Deepak and as we both adjusted to our new circumstances, I got glimpses of this country as he saw it. Through him, I, too, learned about the complexities not only of theorizing and analyzing race/ethnicity, work, and immigration in the United States, but also of navigating them, and living with and in spite of them.

How May I Help You? is a powerful reminder that salespeople and other service workers are, after all, people, in all of their richness and messiness, difference and similarity. The stories found here serve as a chance to humanize debates about work, race, and immigration by taking the time to drink in the United States in the avatar of an electronics store in the South. Here is a take on the United States, familiar and strange, as it seems from the perspective of someone "fresh off the boat"—or, rather, the plane—from a major world civilization, and a country home to fully one-sixth of the world's population, that many people in the United States have imagined as exotic and otherworldly, if they have thought of it at all.

ACKNOWLEDGMENTS

Support came in many forms from many people. First thanks go to my friend Art Collier. He read every page of this book and encouraged me from the first word to the last. I will always remember our discussions at Café Europa, over several afternoons in Charlottesville, Virginia.

I am grateful to anthropologists Susan Blum, Ira Bashkow, and Carolyn Nordstrom, and to the anonymous reviewers for the University of California Press, for providing guidance along the way. Also to fellow writers I met in Ann Arbor, Michigan: Amy Gustine, Ann Epstein, Danielle LaVaque-Manty, Cathy Mellet, Sonja Sirinivasan, Marni Hochman, and Paul Many.

From National Public Radio, I am grateful for the support of Marc Silver and Joe Linstroth. From Public Radio International's *The World*, Marco Werman, Aaron Schachter, and especially Jennifer Goren have helped develop my voice as an essayist and bring my work to a wider audience. I am also indebted to Janis Jaquith and Jill Jaquith for their inspiration and encouragement.

I thank Naomi Schneider for believing in my project. Special thanks to Tamie Parker Song, my brilliant editor. Thanks also to the late Mr. Ram Advani, who fostered my curiosity about books and writing in the Lucknow bookshop where he nurtured writers and readers for over fifty years.

I thank my writer friends of Chelsea Writers' Workshop in Michigan, who read parts of this book: Sandra Xenakis, Michael Kitchen, Shanelle Boluyt, Meg Gower, Lynn McGuire, Michael Andreoni, Deborah Burand, Joan Sampieri, and Brian Cox.

I am deeply grateful to my colleagues, for teaching me not only about selling electronics and surviving the sales floor, but also for opening their hearts and teaching me about the diversity of American lives.

To my parents, my siblings, Pankaj and Gunjan, and my dear friends Shariq Khan and Aftab Ahmad, and to my American family, I wish to express particular gratitude. And to all those I appreciate, but have failed to name, my gratitude and my humble request for forgiveness.

Final and greatest thanks to Holly, with all my love, for making this journey possible.

CHAPTER ONE

Answering Machine

Counting hundreds of dollar bills, rolls of quarters, dimes, nickels, and a fistful of loose change correctly was turning out to be a daunting task. As the clock ticked along, the store phone rang. I answered.

"Aye, listen, I'm comin' to Charlottesville right now. Could you tell me where you guys located at?" Someone spoke in a strangled tongue.

"Yes, sir. We are in the mall."

"I'll be there soon."

It was eight o'clock at night. ElectronicsHut was supposed to close at nine.[1] The lights from the flatscreen TVs skipped on the walls and the grey carpet floor. Jazz played on the home theater system. I stood in the middle of the store, leaning on the counter under the bright fluorescent lights, and looked at everything that surrounded me—radios, antennas, cameras, cables, routers,

---

1. To protect confidentiality, I have changed the names of my workplace and of my colleagues and acquaintances.

scanners, printers, computers, speakers. I was the person in charge of everything in the store for the next hour. Cindy, my boss, a short-haired blonde with average build and big eyes, had left a few minutes ago, telling me, "I'm going home. You'll close today." She knew I was not comfortable with the idea.

"You need to learn to start closing the store on your own. You've been working here long enough," she had told me. "Have a good night. You'll be fine."

Tonight was my first closing shift on my own. I felt nervous. Nervous about not being able to answer a customer's question, not being able to find a product, not being able to handle an irate shopper. Also, I was not sure about counting the money in the cash register at the end of the day. Being responsible for someone else's money made me nervous in general, but being responsible for counting American money, matching the total in the cash register to the one on the computer, and taking thousands of dollars of cash to the bank at night made my misery a hundred times worse.

I had recently arrived in the United States from India, and was still learning American ways. People rolled their eyes when I stared at the coins in my hand, trying to tell a dime from a nickel in an effort to come up with the right change for a donut at a coffee shop. Embarrassed, I'd put the whole chunk of change on the counter and let the cashier pick.

A few minutes later a man wearing a checkered flannel shirt and a pair of light blue jeans walked in with a crumpled plastic bag in his hand. He set it on the counter and pulled out a telephone answering machine.

"It don't work no more. I want my money back," he said in a gruff tone. I knew from his voice that he was the one who had called a few minutes ago. The machine looked worn out. There was no box for it. I asked him if he had the receipt. He pulled out a slip. The print was barely readable. I checked to see the date of purchase. The machine had been bought seven months ago.

"Sir, I'm sorry, but I can't give you the money back. This is past the return period."

"Are you shittin' me? These are supposed to work for a long period of time, not just a few months. C'mon, man, give my money back," he barked.

I didn't know how to react. He reeked of alcohol. He was solidly built, with rough stubby knuckles. He seemed to be in his mid-thirties but had several teeth missing. Numerous thoughts flashed in my mind. In my last job in India, if someone wanted to see me at work, they first had to go through the security guard outside the building, then if the guard thought it was okay, he would let them into the receptionist, who would in turn let me know that there was a visitor. Someone who stank of alcohol and talked in an abusive manner would have never gotten past the burly guard.

But I was not in India. I was standing in front of a drunken man in America, and he was being rude and asking for his money back for something well past its return date. Seven months ago, when he'd purchased the machine, I had no idea that I'd be dealing with an asinine man in Virginia over a product that I didn't know existed.

A part of me wanted to toss his answering machine out the door, rip the sales receipt into pieces and shove it into his stinking mouth. But my job was to treat this guy with respect, talk to him in a professional manner—and, at the same time, not agree to return his money. If I tried to raise my voice, there was a good chance that the customer could hurt me, even pull a gun. If I gave his money back, it was likely that I could lose my job.

I took a deep breath and said, "Sir, I am very sorry, but I can't return your money."

He gave me a cold stare with his hazel eyes and said, "How many gas wells do you own?"

"Excuse me?"

"Tell me, how many gas wells do you own?"

This was the first time someone had ever asked me whether I owned gas wells. I didn't even know what that meant. What did the answering machine have to do with gas wells? I didn't have the faintest clue. I saw saliva frothing around the corner of his quivering lips. He didn't seem like he was going to leave the store without giving me a hard time.

"Let me talk to your manager," he cried.

"She's gone for the night, but she'll be here tomorrow."

He turned around and stomped his feet and let out a few expletives. Then he grabbed a pen from the counter, looked at my nametag and wrote my first name down.

"What's your full name?"

"Deepak Singh."

"I'll be back tomorrow," he pointed at me with the pen.

"Sure."

He put the machine back in the plastic bag and left.

A little after nine, I locked the door to make sure the day was over.

By the time I got home, it was almost ten. My wife and I ate dinner in silence. I could tell she knew I was upset about something and that I didn't feel like talking.

Just when I lay on my bed and closed my eyes, my house phone rang. It was about eleven. No one called me at that time of night except my parents, from India. I answered the phone. To my surprise, it was Cindy. "Deepak, sorry to bother you at this time of the night, but do you know anything about Fallujah?"

At first, I couldn't decide if I was dreaming about work, or if it was really Cindy on the phone.

She had called my home a few times to ask me to come in earlier or to work on my day off because some other employee hadn't shown up, or to ask me where I kept a certain product, or a document that she needed.

It took me a few seconds for her question to register. I said, "What are you looking for, Cindy?"

"Fallujah—do you know where it is?

"Fallujah? No, I don't know, Cindy. But sounds like it could be somewhere in the Middle East."

She cackled and said, "I knew you would know."

"Okay, but why do you ask?"

"Oh, I'm sittin' here watchin' Fox News, and they're talkin' about a suicide bomber who blew himself up in a busy market there." I kept silent. "Hello, you there?"

"Yes."

"Anyway, I'll let you sleep. Oh, by the way, how did last hour go at the store?"

"Do you mind if we talk tomorrow, Cindy? I am very tired."

I laid back in bed and closed my eyes again. I tried to imagine what it might be like for average Americans to work in a retail store in a foreign land without a good grasp of the local language or accent. I tried to picture an educated American working in a corner store in small-town India, selling turmeric, cardamom, cloves, aniseed, peppercorn, cinnamon, fenugreek, mustard, coriander, saffron. And what if this was the only job he could get, even if he had no experience or desire for it, but couldn't quit and return home? How would he fare? How would people treat him?

Then I thought of the time back in Lucknow, when a white American friend of mine asked a cycle rickshaw puller to let him pedal it for a short while. He did that because it was exotic and fun. People stopped to gape at the tourist, a tall man with long hair, pedaling a cycle rickshaw in the place of a scrawny, dark-skinned Indian man. For my friend, it was an adventure of sorts, but the poor Indian man carried people around town, rain or shine, to make sure his family could eat.

I wished working in retail in America were fun and exotic and only lasted for a few minutes—and that I didn't have to depend on it for a living.

CHAPTER TWO

Lucknow

I was born and raised in a Hindu household in Lucknow—a city of four million people in northern India. My hometown is famous for poetry and politeness, and its historical buildings—built by both British and Mughal rulers. I grew up right in the middle of the city and lived in small apartments in compact neighborhoods. Most of my friends lived within a few hundred meters of my home. There were few home phones and no cell phones. If I wanted to see any of my friends, I had to go to their house. They did the same when they wanted to meet me. There was always something going on. A beggar knocking on the door. A vendor hawking a cartful of potatoes. A neighbor asking for sugar. Loud devotional music playing from giant loudspeakers in Shiva's temple across the street. Privacy was something I got only when I was in bed with a sheet over my face. Every once in a while, looking for some peace, I walked or rode my bicycle to the old city and sat for hours on the steps of one of the centuries-old mausoleums.

My father came from a poor family, but he had worked hard to get a college education. His mother had never gone to school and his father was a small-time farmer.

My mother's family was rich. Her father, my Nana, was born in 1926. He was a wealthy landowner who administered several villages under the British rule in India. He spent his growing-up years in a British boarding school in a hill resort town in North India, and came home to his family only during summer vacations. Living in an English environment, he acquired a lot of English mannerisms and tastes, and an English accent. He liked to hunt with his entourage of servants and often drove to the country for hunting expeditions.

My mother often told me this story:

It was a balmy June afternoon in 1955. Your Nana was out with his entourage to hunt for geese. Two men walked behind him carrying birds that he had already shot with his .22, and a couple of people walked ahead of him. They walked for miles in the jungle and kept hunting until it got dark. He took position one more time to get his last kill of the day. He hid behind the bushes and aimed at the geese. The gun went off, but he didn't get the bird. The flutter of the wings and the sound of a loud bang scared a wild bull, which was hiding in the pond. He charged out in a state of panic, keeping his head low, pointing his long horns straight ahead. Your Nana, who wasn't expecting it, and was still kneeling on the ground behind the bush, couldn't get up fast enough to escape, and came in the direct line of the bull's rampage. The bull trampled over his body, injuring his throat badly, and left him in a pool of blood.

His men, who had scampered away in an effort to avoid the bull, returned to see him lying on the ground, unconscious. They carried him to his car and drove him to a hospital, about thirty miles away. Doctors got to work. After an eight-hour surgery, your Nana came out of the emergency room. Doctors said that he was lucky to be alive since most of his throat was cut open, and he had lost a lot of blood. They told his men to take special care of him and only give him liquid foods for the first week.

After four weeks or so, he went to the doctor for his checkup, and got the stitches removed. He looked at himself in the mirror, and felt the scar that ran down his jaw, all the way to the base of his throat. He was ready to hunt again. His people set off with him to find the animal. This time he carried bigger rifles, the ones that he used to kill alligators with. They arrived at the pond and saw the bull submerged, with his hump sticking out. Your Nana gave half a smile and extended his arm towards the man who held the guns, asking for the rifle, one with a double barrel. He loaded it, aimed at the animal, which had no clue what was about to happen, and waited to see its reaction. It raised its head lazily to look at the people staring at him, but didn't move.

Your Nana shot a couple of feet away from the bull, in the middle of the pond. The sound and the sudden ripple in the water caused the animal to run for shelter. As soon as it got out, he fired again. This time he didn't shoot to scare the animal, but to kill it. The bullet hit it in the neck, pretty much in the same spot where it had struck him. The large bull was pushed backward by the force of the bullet. It staggered and tumbled back into the pond. The water turned red. A smile full of content swam across your Nana's face as he handed the gun back to the man standing next to him. The revenge was over.

My mother, who grew up in Faizabad, a smaller city eighty miles from Lucknow, often showed me black-and-white photos from her childhood, including her father's cars. I tried to imagine her life when she was a seven-year-old kid wearing a knee-length dress, playing hopscotch, skipping rope, running around her yard. When she was around twenty-four years old, my Nana put out an advert for his daughter's marriage in the *Times of India*. He was looking for a suitable boy for her—someone educated and employed. My father had taken out an ad for himself in the same newspaper. He was looking for an educated and beautiful girl.

He had a stable job, and my mother was the prettiest woman he had seen. The marriage was quickly arranged. Except for the fact that both my parents were high-caste Hindus, there was not much in common between them. My mother was a devout woman, and my father didn't believe in idol worshipping. My mother followed cricket with a passion, and my father didn't understand the game. My father saw his first Bollywood film at age eighteen. My mother knew the actors like the back of her hand. She grew up in a large bungalow in a city, and my father in a mud house in a dirt-poor village. She went to school in a Vauxhall car. My father walked miles, often barefoot, to an open-air school. She played with her pet Alsatian dogs; my father milked and herded goats. Her father had imported, in 1950s, an Electrolux refrigerator from Sweden so the family could drink cold water during hot months. My father had used a metal bucket to pull water out of a well.

The biggest conflict between my parents was that my father wanted my mother to live in his village to take care of his aging parents. Most of their quarrels went like this:

"I want to send our kids to English-medium, private schools."

"I know you want to turn them into snobs like your own father."

"I just want them to do well and have a good future."

"I didn't even have chairs in my school." My father thought anything better than an open-air school where you didn't have to sit on the floor was a good thing. My parents ended up staying in the city.

Because my mother had gone through so much resistance and criticism from my father and her in-laws for educating us in the city schools, she was extra harsh with her kids. She had a point to prove and she didn't accept any excuse from us for not doing well.

One time, when I was in grade seven or maybe eight, my mother came to the parent-teacher meeting to discuss my performance with many of my teachers. She wasn't impressed with what my teachers had to say about my grades. She listened to all of them, but didn't say anything to me there. When we walked out of the school, she said to me, with fury in her eyes, "If you don't end up fixing punctured tires by the side of the road, I'll change my name."

I looked down.

"You'll be like Ramu, the *puncturewallah*, who didn't graduate from high school. If you get lucky you might become a newspaper delivery man like Sunil." Although she yelled at all three of her kids, she seemed to be most invested in my future.

As years went by, my father also became interested in my education. At some point he realized that I could provide him support—financial, emotional, and physical. I turned twenty-two around the same time that I finished my bachelor's degree. It was an important age. My parents, aunts, and uncles often asked whether I was going to get a job. If I wanted to get a job, then what job? If I wanted to continue studying, another degree must come with the promise of a job, a career. For the first time in my life, I felt I was under pressure. Everyone looked at me as if they were expecting something from me. Even my neighbors asked me, as I walked by, what my plans were.

I, on the other hand, didn't have a clue what I wanted to do. If anything, I wanted to travel. I wanted to get on a train and explore India. India is huge and diverse, and I knew that there was a lot to see. So far, I could count the number of places I had traveled on my two hands. I wanted to travel to the southern parts of India, which are quite different from where I grew up. I wanted to learn another Indian language, immerse myself in a different culture, and eat different kinds of foods. I had once casually presented this idea to my folks and they had looked at me as if I were out of my mind. They had in their minds something very different for me. Two things were required for me to be able to do what I wanted to do: money and my parents' consent. Not obeying your parents was a surefire way of earning a bad reputation among friends and family. I had very little money and no approval from them.

During the first year of getting my bachelor's degree, I had lied to my parents that I was going to spend a week with my friend in a neighboring town. I actually went to Nainital—a popular hill station—about three hundred miles from Lucknow. I was only nineteen then. My friend, a son of a wealthy bureaucrat, had arranged free food and lodging for us in a government guesthouse. I only had to come up with a few hundred rupees for train tickets and food along the way. We took the train to Haldwani, a small town and the closest railway station to our destination. There we boarded a government bus, which soon began its ascent on the narrow roads that snaked up and around the mountainous terrain. The higher we climbed the cooler it got. Clouds floated below us. It was October. Bobby and I arrived in Nainital around six in the evening. A couple of hours earlier and several thousand feet below, it had been hot and muggy. When we got off the bus, a cold draft hit my face. It was dusk and there was still a hint of blue in the sky. Below it were tall mountains with shimmering lights. Right in the middle was the lake, reflecting the lights from the mountains. I immediately fell in love with the place.

While I was gone, my father and mother found out that I had lied and gone to Nainital. There was no way for them to track me down; there were no cell phones, and very few people had home phones. They had asked around and gotten in touch with a few friends of mine who knew about my whereabouts. They couldn't do anything except to wait. When I returned, my family looked at me with mixed emotions. My father lowered his head. He didn't say anything, but he seemed both happy and disappointed—happy that I was back, sad that I had left without telling him. My mother looked angry. She told me how much my father had harassed her for what I had done. "This is what you get when you give your kids English education," he had repeatedly told her.

I had gotten away with it when I was nineteen, but now I was twenty-two. They wanted me to hurry up and figure what I wanted to do next. I wasn't alone. All my classmates and friends were busy planning or had already decided what they wanted to do. Since my bachelor's degree was in commerce, the obvious thing to go for was an MBA. In 1995, a postgraduate degree came with a lot of prestige and promise. There weren't many institutions that offered an MBA program. The ones that did were very hard to get into. Quite a few of my father's friends suggested I should prepare for the entrance exam. I didn't think I was cut out to be a corporate honcho, but I didn't know enough to really know.

Growing up, when I was seven or maybe eight, when people asked me what I wanted to be when I grew up, I said, "a singer." When I was ten, I said I wanted to be a musician. I kept a harmonica under my pillow every night. Around the same time, I also aspired to be a painter. Sitting by the window, painting dark clouds and green trees was my favorite pastime during hot months. My parents encouraged me, or at least didn't laugh at my ideas when I was that age, probably thinking I'd grow out of my fantasies. If I'd seen a way to become a singer and earn a livelihood, I might have pursued that passion. But my singing talent never made it out of the bathroom. I continued playing harmonica as an amateur, though.

So, I did what seemed like the best idea at the time. I applied for business school. The results for the exam were declared soon, but I didn't have the courage to look at the list myself. I sent my younger brother to see whether my name was on the list. He came back with a blank expression. Looking at his face, I knew I hadn't been chosen. He walked into the house without saying anything. No one said anything. Then he jumped on me and yelled, "You made it!"

It was a big deal for my family, not only because I had been selected from a large pool of thousands of candidates, but also because my parents had to come up with a great sum of money to pay the fees. Back in the early nineties in India, an MBA was a surefire way to get a highly paid job and a lot of prestige. My mother was ready to sell all her jewelry to make sure I could go to school. My father was not 100 percent sure that was a good idea. He had to marry off my sister. He had some savings, which he had planned to use for her wedding.

My family thought about it for several days. We had about a week to decide. My father decided to borrow some money and to dig into his lifelong savings. I felt bad, almost guilty, that he had to do that. I felt that my family was going through this only because my name was among the list of selected candidates. It was a big strain for my folks, but as time went on, they seemed happy about their decision. During the two years that I was in business school, they never stopped talking about me to people.

When I started the program, I met students from all parts of India. This was a first for me. Everyone I had gone to school with until now, I had known since childhood. We had all gone to the same secondary school, same coaching classes, same university. In business school, I met people who had very different educational backgrounds. Folks with degrees in engineering, law, education, sociology, and history. Some of them were quite a bit older than me and had several years of work experience. There were engineers who wanted a business degree to advance in their career. There were schoolteachers who wanted to change careers. And there were people who wanted to get an MBA so they could manage their family business or start their own venture. I had never studied with such a diverse group of people. I wasn't sure if I belonged there. I wasn't sure if I could handle the pressure to perform.

The competition, from the day one, was fierce. Almost every other day, we had to present a paper before the class of sixty students. I found it nerve-wracking to stand up and speak and answer everyone's questions, knowing that 20 percent of our grades depended on how well we presented our paper. This was in 1995. Internet hadn't reached India yet. Wikipedia was years away from being created. We worked hard to conduct our research on various topics. One of our classmates had a personal computer and a printer at her house and everyone hated her for that. She was the one who typed and printed her papers and assignments. Most of us wrote with our own hands. It cost a lot of money to go to a shop to get our work typed and printed.

I couldn't keep up with the assignments. No matter how hard I worked, I was always behind on something. One day I came home, overwhelmed with work and pressure, and lay on the bed. My mother asked me, "What's wrong? Are you okay?"

"Can I quit?"

"Quit what?" she said with a curious face.

"MBA."

She looked at me for a few seconds and said, "Can I slap your face?" The conversation ended.

She knew I was working hard and struggling. She couldn't help me with work at school, but wanted to make sure I was healthy. She made me drink a glass of milk every night. It was her way of supporting me, providing me strength, mental and physical.

I carried on with the program, but my heart wasn't there. I couldn't bring myself to fall in love with any of the courses. Oftentimes while attending a lecture in organizational behavior or industrial marketing, or statistics, I thought, "Why?" Sitting next to some of my friends in class, I watched them frenetically jotting down every word that came out of the professor's mouth. What was I missing, I wondered?

In the two years I was in business school, I was gone from nine in the morning to six at night, and when I got home I was drowned in homework. I didn't have much time to hang out with my friends in the building. I had stopped playing cricket. This caused a lot of my friends to think I was avoiding them, or I didn't want to associate with them. People started to behave differently with me. My friends envied me. Kids and teenagers looked up to me. They came to me to get advice about their careers. They wanted me to help them write essays in English. Mothers talked about me, smiled and gave me a flutter of their hands, leaning on the railings of their balconies. "He's the one who got selected in an MBA program," I heard them saying. This made my parents happy. For them, this was worth all the money they were spending on me.

I finished my degree. Everyone in my class wanted a corporate job, but I wasn't sure. I couldn't envision myself wearing a necktie to work every day. I spent several months figuring out what I wanted to do. And, one day, I met a media consultant from England who thought I would make a good radio journalist. He offered me a job in the BBC World Service in my hometown. I had grown up listening stories about how my grandfather and my mother listened to BBC on their crackly radios in the 1950s. I had never imagined working for the company.

After I'd worked for a month, the accountant gave out monthly paychecks to all the employees. My turn came and he called me to his desk, and made me sign on a sheet of paper. Then he handed me the check. The amount on it said fifteen thousand rupees, three hundred dollars, just as big as my father's monthly wage. I thanked the accountant and moved away from his desk. I came out of the office and checked to see whether the check was really for me. For someone who had spent almost a quarter of a century living on an allowance of five hundred rupees, ten dollars a month, a paycheck that was as big as my dad's—who supported a family of five—was hard to come to terms with.

I was excited and didn't know what to do with it. Several outrageous ideas of how to spend it flashed through my mind. I went to the restroom several times that day to take the check out, feel with my fingers how *my* name was printed on it. I tried to contain my emotions, calm down, and not go crazy.

The day at work came to an end. I reached home, ran up the three flights of stairs without stopping, pushed the doorbell and held it down until someone answered. My dad opened the door and saw me standing there, panting. He asked whether I was okay. Since I was out of breath, I didn't say anything, but showed him my paycheck. He looked at it, and gestured to me to come in to the living room. My mother and sister were sitting on the couch against the wall, watching the TV in the corner. Right next to the TV were two chairs, beside a settee. I sat down on one of the chairs, next to my father. Slanted sunrays entered through the large windows behind the settee and brought my face into focus.

I smiled and exclaimed, "I can buy the new Honda motorbike now."

My dad took the check out of my hands and said, "Are you stupid? You want to buy a motorcycle? Who's going to pay off the loan I took out for your MBA? Who's going to pay the mortgage for the land we bought? Who's going to pay for your sister's wedding?"

After he fired several questions at me, he calmed down and looked at me. I looked at my mother, my sister, my brother, and then back at my father, as if they were the audience in a court watching me, the accused, and my father, the judge. When I didn't respond to any of his questions, he answered all of them with just one word: "You."

I was back to getting a monthly allowance—my dad felt generous and raised it to one thousand rupees, twenty dollars, since I was earning now. He took most of my money every month and asked me to inform him dutifully of any raises or bonuses that I might get.

The fact that my dad owned my paycheck every month didn't make a huge difference in my lifestyle or responsibilities. I was still my parents' little kid—I just had a job now and instead of taking money from them, I was giving money to them.

They never thought of it as a great favor. They saw it as a role reversal—they had taken care of me for twenty-some years, and now it was my turn. The only problem I had with the arrangement was that I was not learning how to run a house or a family.

I was contributing my salary, but I didn't have to take on full responsibility; other people still paid bills, bought groceries, cooked food, repaired the car. My parents did some of these things. Sometime we hired help. My responsibilities were simply to go to work and come home.

Soon after I got the job, my father's colleagues and friends started showing up at our door with marriage proposals for me. My father told them that he was in no rush to marry me off, but his friends didn't stop coming.

One evening when I returned from work, I found a potbellied, bespectacled middle-aged man sitting in our living room. I knew exactly why he was there. I avoided him, but my father got me to come and sit with them. Reluctantly, I joined them. The man asked me questions about how much money I was making, and if I was going to get a raise soon. Then he pulled out a picture from his shirt pocket and said, "This is Smita. My daughter."

I looked at the picture with a fine balance of interest and disinterest and then rested it on the coffee table. Then he gave me a piece of paper. "This is her bio data," he said. I was absolutely sure in my mind that I wouldn't marry his daughter. I looked at the bio data, a resume, and smiled, but didn't say anything. He didn't say anything either. After a few minutes of awkward silence, I left the room.

This became a routine. Every other day, I would find some man sitting in our home waiting for me. When it got to be too much, I called home from work to see if anyone was there to meet me. If someone was there, I would stay out longer.

While my parents were busy looking for a nice upper-caste Hindu girl, I was trying to enjoy unmarried life as much I could. One of my favorite pastimes was to walk up and down the entire length of Hazratganj—a half-mile stretch of a street with swanky restaurants, movie theaters, libraries, and shops that sold clothes, perfume, handicrafts, books, and music. Every day after sundown beautiful ladies walked in the corridors of Hazratganj, leaving a trail of scent that caused men to forget what they had come to shop for.

In Hazratganj, above an historic theater, the Mayfair, there was a British library that I had been a member of for as long as I could remember. It cost less than eight dollars for an entire year's membership, and had books on a variety of subjects, videotapes about life in the UK, and audiotapes of several British radio dramas. My favorite was a radio comedy program, *The Goon Show*. I would put on the headphones, close my eyes, and pretend that I was not in Lucknow, but in 1960s London, surrounded by a bunch of crazy Englishmen speaking Cockney.

One day, on one of my visits to the library, I saw a brown-haired, green-eyed girl. Intrigued, I walked up to her and introduced myself and asked where she was from.

"America," she said. Her name was Holly. It was rare to see Westerners in Lucknow. I was surprised to learn that Holly was planning to stay in Lucknow for a year. I invited her for a cup of tea, to which she agreed.

Holly told me she was from western Pennsylvania. I had never heard of Pennsylvania before. I tried to imagine the place as something from the scenes in the American movies—*Home Alone, Miami Blues, Face Off, Blue Lagoon*, and a few other Hollywood flicks—that I had watched at the Mayfair. My knowledge of America was limited.

Holly had just finished her undergrad from a liberal arts college in Ohio. She was spending a year in Lucknow on a Fulbright scholarship doing research on history. She wanted to learn about the city, its culture, and the language. I took her to my favorite chai shop, which was quite basic, but had delicious chai and was unpretentious. We sat on wooden benches under squeaky ceiling fans and drank chai that was served in tiny glass mugs. I liked her laidback attitude. She seemed like a girl I could spend a lot of time with.

A few days later I took her home to meet my parents, sister, and brother.

My mother, a gregarious woman, hit it off with Holly from day one. Holly started showing up at my home quite often. She became friends with my family. She was staying in a girls-only hostel in Lucknow and had to be back in her room before eight. She didn't like that, since we liked to hang out in the evenings. Our meetings became more frequent and she decided to move to a different place in Lucknow, a place that didn't have any time limitation. I found her a place, a room in a bungalow that was central and safe. A friend—a septuagenarian woman—owned it, and that meant I could come and go as I pleased. In the new place we had more freedom and we slowly became more than friends.

Her year in India came to an end and it was time for her to return. She didn't want to leave. I didn't want her to go. We were not sure what to do. Holly decided to go back to the United States with a heavy heart. She told me she wanted to see whether she still had the same feelings for me from ten thousand miles away.

It was quite hard for both of us to be apart, but I think it was harder for me, at least in the beginning, since I was still in the same place, the same city, and there were so many things that reminded me of her absence, the void. The chai shop, the bungalow she lived in, and several other places where we spent time.

When she returned to the States, we started chatting on Hotmail messenger. The Internet was a new thing in India in the late nineties. Cybercafes were a new business and there were often long lines to use a computer. I became a regular customer at the Internet cafe close to my home. To make sure I had a computer to myself, I often got there a several minutes before I was supposed to start chatting. When Holly came online, we chatted for hours. Once in a while, we called each other, but we mostly relied on the Internet since it was much cheaper. During this time, Holly had been accepted into a doctoral program in anthropology at the University of Virginia. As time passed, and because both of us didn't know when exactly we were going to meet again, we often wondered about where our relationship was going.

Then about a year later, when we were chatting, she surprised me.

"Can you handle this?' the words appeared on the little square box on my computer screen.

"What?" I asked.

"I am coming to Lucknow again! This time on a different scholarship," she typed.

I quickly logged off and called her number in America. I am not sure exactly how much my bill was that night, but it burned a big hole in my pocket. It was worth it, though. I couldn't wait to see her again.

When she arrived this time, we decided to get engaged. When I proposed the idea to my parents, they were taken aback at first. This is not what they had planned for me. They had never thought that I would bring a foreign bride home, but it didn't completely shock them since they had witnessed my relationship with Holly unfold. Apart from the fact that she wasn't my parents' idea of a typical *bahu,* an Indian daughter-in-law, they had grown to like her.

Holly and I married in a traditional Hindu wedding. I tried to keep the wedding small by Indian standards. Only 150 people were invited, instead of 1,000.

We went to a beach for our honeymoon in eastern India, on the Bay of Bengal. It was there that I saw the ocean for the first time. We stayed in a hotel right on the beach. We walked for hours on the seashore, drew a heart on the sand with our names in it, and drank lots of coconut water. But, soon it was time to be separated again. She had to return to America, and I didn't want to leave my job. I was torn between the choices: keeping my job or joining my wife in Charlottesville, Virginia.

A lot of my friends and colleagues told me I would have no problem finding a similar job in the United States. I spoke English well and had BBC World Service on my CV. Some others said, "Be prepared. America can also be a rude shock."

I quit my job in India and bought a one-way ticket to Washington, DC.

CHAPTER THREE

Transit

It was my first international journey. As I packed my suitcase, I kept noticing new items in it. My mother was rearranging it every few hours, adding a jar of her homemade mango pickle or a box filled with medicines in case I got a headache, flu, or indigestion. I noticed there were a couple tubes of toothpaste and a few bars of soap. I didn't question her, but it seemed as if she was thinking I might return before the soap or toothpaste ran out. I didn't want to make her sad by reminding her that I was traveling on a one-way ticket.

My father bought me thermal underwear and said, "Never step out of the house without wrapping up well." He shoved a wad of cash in my shirt pocket. He looked away as he said, "I know this is not much, but this is all I have right now." He didn't want to show me his wet eyes. With a heavy heart, I left my home in Lucknow.

I cleared all the formalities at the Indira Gandhi International Airport, in New Delhi. I remember the date—September 9, 2003. As I sat waiting at the gate, the various events that had led to this day dawned on me. I was actually moving to the United States.

As I write this, I wonder what I, the Deepak who has lived in the United States for more than a decade, would say to the Deepak that was waiting at the New Delhi airport to come to America for the first time. I would not discourage him from coming to the United States, but I would tell him the realistic picture. That the America he is going to see in person is very different from the America he has seen in Hollywood movies in India. Yes, even janitors own a car in the United States, but not because they can afford one, but because they can't afford to not own one. Yes, Indians are among the most successful immigrants in the United States, but not all Indians, or immigrants in general, own motels and businesses and become doctors. There are Indians who mop the floors and clean the toilets and struggle to pay their rent. America has the world's best health system, but it's not available to everyone. I would also tell him—myself—to leave behind any ego, arrogance, or privilege that he might have had in India.

Soon, I heard the announcement. It was time to board the Austrian Airlines plane. As soon as I stepped on the plane, it seemed as though I were already in a foreign land. The smiling, all-white aircraft crew greeted everyone in German-accented English. Very few people looked like me. The thought that this giant metal box was going to fly in a few minutes made me nervous and more than a little unsure. A part of me wanted to get off and take the next train back to Lucknow.

It was about 10 at night. I settled into a seat and thought of my parents. My father would probably be in bed, but my mother and brother would still be watching TV for a while before they slept. They also ate their dinner late. My brother controlled the remote and my mother watched what he wanted to watch, which was usually a cricket match. If I had been sitting next to him, I'd have been watching the same thing, slapping his knee or shouting at the screen. Everyone in my family except my father could watch cricket any time of day.

I found the menu in the back pocket of the airplane seat. Among the many choices, I could recognize only one item: samosa. Soon, the aircraft took off. Out my window, I saw the twinkling lights of Delhi fading away from me as the plane soared. Slowly, everything turned into darkness, as if India were turning off its lights for the night, saying goodnight to me. I rested my head on the window, straining my eyes to see the last glimmer, and then faded to sleep. The next time I opened my eyes, the captain was telling us we were descending into Vienna.

I walked around the airport looking for a pay phone to call home. But all the cafes, souvenir shops, and payphones accepted only euros. The only currencies I had on me were dollars and rupees. I walked some more, clutching the bag that had my passport, visa papers, and money. I had heard stories of immigration officers in America deporting people back to their country if they didn't have the required documents. I was both sleepy and fearful.

Soon, it was time to get on the plane again. I was happily surprised to see a young Indian man sitting next to me. We smiled at each other, but he only spoke Punjabi, not any English or Hindi, the two languages I knew. Luckily, I had acquired a few words in Punjabi during my two years working at the BBC for a British Sikh boss who swore in Punjabi when he was angry. Like me, my new friend on the plane was traveling to the States for the first time. He said he already had a job; his uncle owned a car repair shop and he was going to help him. Although his English was nonexistent, he seemed very relaxed and confident. When I asked him what kind of visa he had, he said he didn't know, but he had a bunch of documents in a manila envelope. He told me his uncle had sponsored him a long time ago and he had been waiting for this day for the last ten years.

I felt sorry for the guy and wondered how he would manage in America without English. It made me feel good about myself. I silently thanked my mother who had made sure I went to good English-language schools. A degree in business administration, work experience in a company of international repute, fluency in English—I imagined myself landing a good job soon after arriving in the States. I couldn't wait tell my parents.

After a few hours, I heard the pilot declare that we were getting ready to descend into the American capital. I looked through the window and saw the sun sitting low in the sky. The houses appeared like tiny dots neatly marked in rows. The plane was low and I could see vehicles on wide streets moving in an orderly fashion. One of these cars could contain Holly, I thought excitedly, coming to get me from the airport.

I smiled as I heard the thud. The wheels had touched down on American soil! I got off and followed the directions along the hallway. There were different sections for different travelers— permanent residents, U.S. citizens, and visa holders. I got in a line that was moving slowly compared to the others. People with green cards and U.S. passports had an easy time going through immigration. Every person in my line was spending several minutes at the counter. Would the officer ask me a lot of questions? Would he be able to understand my accent? What if he sent me back to India? Or would he take pity on me and let me go through? After torturing myself for twenty minutes, my turn came and the officer gestured me to come up to him.

I presented him with my papers. Without looking at me, he asked me to put my finger on a machine. He asked me a few questions in a matter-of-fact tone and I answered, trying my best to stay calm. He looked at me again, flipped through my passport a few more times, looking bored, and then gave it back. "You're good to go," he said.

My luggage didn't show up immediately, but I was unusually calm. I knew I was going to walk out of the airport and into the United States, with or without my luggage, and no one was going to stop me.

In a few minutes, my suitcases came tumbling through the carousel, looking beat up and bruised. I loaded them on a cart and started pushing. Airport authorities dressed in dark-blue uniforms carried walkie-talkies in their hands. Loudspeakers were announcing flights to Atlanta, San Francisco, Chicago, and New York. Hearing the names of the cities I had fantasized about visiting one day was surreal. I could go to any of those cities. All I needed was a plane ticket. I didn't need a visa. I was already inside America.

Holly had told me that she was going to be an hour late because of her class. When I finally saw her, she was wearing a yellow top and blue jeans and had her sunglasses on her head. It was magical. I had traveled more than ten thousand miles from Lucknow to New Delhi to Vienna to Washington, DC and was now in the waiting lounge of Dulles International Airport. There were a lot of things that could have gone wrong along the way, but somehow my Holly, the same Holly I was in love with, the same Holly I had spent endless hours with in chai shops in Lucknow, the same Holly I was married to, was now standing before me—in the United States of America. I had never seen her in jeans in India. I continued staring at her from happiness and wonder. She was the same woman, but she was not the same woman. I hugged her and wanted to kiss her on the lips, but I thought it would be inappropriate to indulge in public display of affection. My jetlagged mind should have figured out that I wasn't in India anymore, and that it was okay to kiss.

We walked out of the airport, and I took a deep breath. Twenty-four hours earlier, outside Indira Gandhi International Airport in New Delhi, the air had felt thick. American air felt crisp and fresh.

Holly had driven her Oldsmobile sedan from Charlottesville to pick me up. We walked toward the parking lot and I found myself in a maze of cars. I had never seen so many cars at one time in one place. Many the brands I had heard of and seen only in the movies were now right before my eyes—Porsche, Cadillac, Lincoln, Buick. Holly asked me to find her car. I had seen it in pictures, but that didn't help. I looked around and saw a trunk opening in the distance. I looked at my wife and she smiled. I noticed the remote in her hand.

I walked up to it and saw the back of the vehicle. The trunk was so big that I had to bend down to see how deep it was. I put my two suitcases and the handbag in it, but it had room for at least four more. I remembered the Indian saying, *Oont ke muh me jeera*. It means tossing a tiny seed in a camel's mouth. I tried to open the door to get in and Holly said, "Are you going to drive?"

"Don't you know I can't drive?" I said, wondering if she was serious.

"Well, then, get in on the passenger's side." She smiled.

I looked into the car and saw the steering wheel on the left. For the last thirty years of my life, I had seen cars with steering wheels on the right-hand side. It was second nature to me to walk to the left side of the car to sit in the front passenger's seat. At first glance, seeing the steering wheel on the left was almost like seeing a human being with a nose on his forehead.

I came around to the right and opened the door. The eight-inch-thick solid-metal door felt heavier than both my suitcases put together. Inside, I noticed the vastness of the dashboard. It was big enough to be a dining table for a family of five. Holly and I were separated by a massive hand rest. I stretched my legs out all the way, which I hadn't been able to do since New Delhi, and they still couldn't reach the front of the car. The seat was so big that I could comfortably ride with another person in it. And then I looked behind me. The backseat was like a different room in this hotel-suite of a car. It was bigger and plusher than the couch in my parents' home. I could have easily played cricket in the space between the front seat and backseat. I wondered about the size of the car and why Holly needed it, especially when she was the only one using it.

"My grandparents bought it for me. They wanted me to be safe," she told me, focusing on the road. It was strange to hear this from her since she had never said anything about safety when she rode on the back of my scooter without a helmet on the streets full of stray dogs, cows, and crazy drivers in Lucknow.

While I was still thinking, she said, "Can you look over your shoulder to see if I can change lanes?"

I looked over and told her it was clear. Compared to the side-view mirror on my scooter in Lucknow, which I never used, the mirror on this car was the size of a little television. I asked her why she didn't use that instead.

"I hate driving on the highway," she explained.

As we went along, I gaped at the giant WALMART, FED EX, and McDONALD's signs painted on the many vehicles that passed us. America! I thought.

Somewhere along the way the exhaustion from the journey got the better of me. When I woke up, I saw Holly outside the window, holding a nozzle at a gas station. I rubbed my eyes and stepped out. There was another car next to ours. There was a man sitting inside, shaking his head to loud and offensive music. The sound from his car was vibrating the hood of our car. The music was the only sound I had heard so far on our trip from the airport. I was used to listening to loud honks on the streets of Lucknow, but had never heard songs with swear words in them.

We got on our way again. The music had chased the sleep away from me. I sat up in my seat and looked out the window, thinking that I was seeing a very different side of Holly. She was authoritative and in control. Back in Lucknow, I was responsible for doing things like driving my scooter, filling up the gas, haggling for a better price with a shopkeeper. She rode behind me and I drove. I had seen a lot of women drive in India, but I had never seen a woman actually getting out of the car to fill up the gas. They always gestured from inside their cars to the guy manning the pump. The man in an oil-stained uniform filled up the gas and the customer paid in cash without stepping out of the vehicle. Even men stayed inside their cars. It was a sort of a privilege that car owners enjoy in India. Watching Holly holding the nozzle at the pump was a sort of a kick to the head that said, "Of course! This is America!"

I half-smiled and then thought about my own vulnerability. I didn't even know how to drive a car, and I knew that at some point I'd have to learn to maneuver this beast of an Oldsmobile.

I gave Holly a worried look. She said, "Don't worry, we're not too far from Charlottesville."

It was getting dark. I touched the window and it felt cold. I rolled the glass down and then quickly rolled it back up. September in Virginia felt as cold as December in Lucknow. The roads now were only two lanes wide and the speed limit had dropped to fifty-five. Soon I saw a sign that said *Welcome to Charlottesville.*

Holly flicked on her left indicator and we made a turn into a smaller street. Soon she turned into a driveway and parked the car. Lights came on. We were now in front of a red brick house, the same house that Holly had shown me in pictures when we were in India. I got out of the car and saw the sign, "615" on top of the door. It was the same number I had been writing on envelopes to send letters to Holly from India. It was hard to believe that I was standing before it.

There was a small grassy patch in front of the house and a slightly bigger yard behind the house. Holly shared the house with a couple other people. I walked into the house, hoping to see others. No one was there. I asked who had turned on the lights outside. "Oh, they're automatic," said Holly. Though I had never seen automatic lights before, I smiled as if to say, "Of course."

Holly took me into the kitchen. There was a four-burner electric stove. Each burner looked like the small electric heater in my parents' home in Lucknow, the one that we used to keep warm during winter months and sometimes cooked on, but that we couldn't rely on for most of our cooking because of the frequent power cuts. Instead, we used gas stoves for almost all of our cooking. I took another look at the electric stove. There were four ON knobs on the front panel to control the heat and an exhaust fan built into the back. I found it hard to believe that an electric stove could be used as the main device for cooking.

"This stove wouldn't be very practical in India," I said.

"I know. It's okay, because power outages are rare here."

I turned around and saw the sink. There were two knobs on it. I turned on the first one. Cold water gushed out of the faucet. Then I turned on the other one, and had to jerk my hand back.

"Yep, it's hot. Be careful," Holly said. "Hot water is good for washing dishes." In India, we never used hot water for washing the dishes. The only time we used hot water was on the rare occasions when it got too cold to bathe with cold water. We boiled big pots of water on the gas stove and mixed it with the tap water for bucket baths. It was a lot of bother and time consuming to boil several pots of water; I had gotten used to the cold water. Pouring the first mug on your head was the hardest. I usually took a deep breath and closed my eyes then doused myself with the icy water. The rest was easy. I waited to take a bath until the sun came out. Standing under the sun was a good way to warm up.

I noticed another knob above the sink. Out of curiosity, I flicked it on. I had to cover my ears immediately. A loud noise filled the house. Holly quickly turned it off.

"That's the garbage disposal unit."

"What does that do?"

"It crushes the food waste so the drain doesn't get clogged."

I looked at the knob again and made sure I knew it well, although I was too jetlagged to think clearly. Holly, new country, new place to live, new environment—everything seemed different.

I noticed there were no light bulbs on the ceilings or the walls. Instead, there were lamps in each corner. Then I looked up. Standing on my toes, I could almost touch the ceiling. I had never been inside a house with this low a ceiling. Growing up in a hot climate, I'd only ever been in houses designed to accommodate ceiling fans. Once, putting on my shirt while standing on my bed, my mother had yelled at me, "Watch your hand!" I was only an inch away from the fan.

While I was still taking in everything, Holly brought me a cordless phone. "You should call your parents and let them know you've arrived." She had bought twenty dollars worth of minutes for me to call home, which I thought it was very nice of her.

I heard my mother's voice at the other end. I had never spoken to my mother from so far away. When I told her that I had just reached the United States, she got quiet. After a pause she said, "Did you have your breakfast?" I told her it was dinnertime in America.

"We are getting ready to have breakfast here. I have made *parathas,* but—" I could tell my mother was trying her best not to cry. I got quiet, too.

"What are you going to eat for dinner?" she asked.

"I don't know. I just got here."

"I don't know if you'll like the food." She was worrying about my dinner from ten thousand miles away. I didn't know what to tell her except that I'd be okay, although a part of me wished I were having *parathas* in Lucknow. I was having trouble keeping myself from crying. I didn't want her to hear that. I told her I had to finish unpacking and that I'd call her the next morning.

"Look after yourself," she said. Holly held my hand and gave me a hug. I was tired, sad, and happy, all at the same time. We lay on the bed together, but a lot of things were on my mind. Holly was the reason I had given up my Indian life. I worried, for the first time in my relationship with her, that I might not have done the right thing. What if I didn't like her American avatar? What if she didn't like me in America? I had these questions on my mind on that first night and I was years away from finding out the answers. I fell asleep soon.

CHAPTER FOUR

My American Wife

"This is so cool," said Holly, looking at the shiny pressure cooker I had brought for her from India. Her exclamation of the word *cool* took me by surprise. There was something about Holly's reaction, the way she said it, juxtaposed against the Indian-ness of the pressure cooker, that caught me off guard. I had never heard her speak like that.

In India, Indians often commented how Indian her English was. Now I began to notice her accent. It sounded harsher than I remembered. Her *T*s were more like *D*s and her *R*s sounded grating to my ear. I wasn't a big fan of the way she said "man" at the end or the beginning of nearly every sentence. And often she said "man" with nothing before and nothing after it. There was something belittling about it, but I wasn't completely sure why I didn't like it. The innocence and the sweetness of Holly's voice, her demure manner that I had fallen in love with, were missing.

I was getting strange vibes from her. She wasn't acting the same as she had in India. This caused me to be more uptight around her than I had ever been. I was expecting her to behave like the Holly I had known in my country. I was aware that that might not be the case, but I also expected her to be a little more supportive than I thought she was. I knew she was the only person I could ask questions, and I had thousands of them. I had stepped into a different world, literally different, and I felt like I needed help at every step, and for the most mundane of things. I asked her about which shampoo to use in the shower—there were four different kinds and all of them belonged to different people. I asked her about the TV channels since there were a hundred more than on my cable network in India. I asked her about where to get a haircut and about everything else I didn't know. She gave me curt answers, and her tone was often dismissive.

This was the first time I was going to live in a city where I didn't know anyone except Holly. This was the first time I was going to live in a house that didn't belong to my parents or me. There was nothing in the house that was familiar to me—the smells, the sounds, the layout. I couldn't move without letting everyone in the house know that I was moving. The floor squeaked every time I yawned. The walls smelled like coffee—no trace of cloves and cardamom. It felt as if no one had ever boiled a pot of chai in the house. Before this, I had never been inside a kitchen that didn't have yellow turmeric stains from cooking *daal*.

I wondered about a lot of items in the house. The array of wine and liquor bottles—which were all *sharaab*, alcohol, to me. I didn't know who consumed so much alcohol. My father had been an alcoholic at some point, but even then he drank only one bottle a day. Why were there twenty bottles in a house of three people? I would find out soon.

Within days of arriving in that house, I began to feel unwelcome. Not so much by Holly, but by the other housemates. They were not thrilled to have another person living in the house.

There were three bedrooms in the house, and according to them, there was only enough room for three members, not four. Holly had told me this so I tried to confine myself to our room. I thought it would help if I didn't have to show my face to them. I became so conscious of myself that I stopped making chai or cooking *parathas* in the kitchen. I didn't want the smell of Indian food to remind them of my presence. I even removed my black hairs from the wet walls after my shower.

Holly often left me in the room and went to talk to folks downstairs. She told me she didn't want others to think that she had abandoned her friends. It angered me that she thought it was okay for her to abandon *me*. I had no friends and back in the early 2000s it was expensive to call India. I couldn't just pick up the phone and talk to friends or family. One day when I was alone at home, I used the house phone to call my cousin in Toronto. I was unhappy and it was nice to talk to him. He had been in Canada for a while and he could relate to what I was going through. About a week later, the telephone bill came. It was much higher than usual.

"Who called Canada?" everyone asked. When I said that it was me, they made Holly pay the difference in the bill. She wasn't happy about it. She understood why I called my cousin, but told me not to do this again.

Little things like that started to get to me. As the days passed, I got desperate. I wanted to get my work permit and start working. My money had run out. I would walk into a store, and out of impulse pick up a can of soda or a cookie, and then put it back, realizing that I couldn't pay for it. I had never been this destitute in my life.

I was beginning to get depressed. At home, there were parties twice a week. Holly's friends and housemates gathering over food and wine. The parties would start around seven in the evening and go until two in the morning. The people started out talking about anthropology, travel, music, food, and American sitcoms. Before everyone got drunk, they asked me how I was doing, adjusting, but after they had downed a couple of glasses of wine, they didn't even notice I was there. They would talk about some video game they had played in their childhood, some American TV show they had grown up watching. I was often a piece of furniture at the house parties.

A lot of wine flowed at these parties, which was new to me. Watching Holly sit with her friends, both men and women, bothered me. I would sit and look at her and not say anything. I felt insecure seeing her sit next to muscular white men, not protesting, but giggling, as the glasses around the table filled and emptied more than once. The whole scene made me feel like throwing wine in someone's face.

As the parties would progress and the wine bottles empty, people got loud and nonsensical. They talked about sex with gusto. To be polite and social, I sat with them, but soon I grew bored and impatient. In my high school years, my male friends had joked about penises or vaginas, but never when girls were around. I found it hard to get the tofu they served down my throat when I heard ladies talk about their sexual fantasies with men whom they'd just met. The house smelled like wine, and I developed a dislike for it. I often excused myself and went into our room and lay on the bed. Holly continued to sit with her friends. I clenched my teeth in frustration when I heard men guffawing and women shrieking at crude jokes.

I doubted my decision to marry an American woman. Quitting my job in India and moving to America seemed like a mistake. I had emptied my bank account to pay for the plane ticket, visa fees, and everything else needed to come to the United States. Lying on a futon bed, my hands on my chest, I stared at the ceiling and thought that I had nothing to go back to. I couldn't even tell my parents what I was going through. Describing the scene in the house to them would be reaffirming their suspicions about my decision. I had no friends or relatives in America. I felt so alone.

Looking back now, I feel bad for Holly—a twenty-five-year-old grad student who had a tiny stipend to support herself and, now, me. She had lectures to go to, talks to attend, and fat books to read for her classes. And then she had to babysit me. She had never lived with a man, let alone an Indian man who had come to America for the first time. Having me around in the house had also changed how her friends acted towards her. They thought that I had stolen her from them.

My wife had grown up in a very small town in rural Pennsylvania, and had done a lot of odd jobs when she was younger. Very few people in her family had gone to college. She was the smartest kid in her village, that's what folks in her family told me, but Holly told me she didn't have the confidence, the sense of entitlement, that other students at her college had. She had secured admission with a scholarship at Kenyon College, a top-rated private liberal arts school in rural Ohio.

Her family spent the night in their car when they first arrived to drop her off for freshman orientation. They couldn't afford to get a hotel for the night. As a newcomer in America, I had failed to understand that people could be so poor in the wealthiest country on earth. In college she had a roommate who said things like, "My parents are just barely managing to send my brother and I to college and to take us on vacation to France after final exams. Can't wait for this semester to end."

To that she gave a short, supportive answer along the lines of, "Yeah, cool, it'll be done soon," but she seethed inside, thinking, *Not only do I have to do well this semester, but I have to pack up, go home, and get to work at Sheetz all summer making coffee and hoagies and ringing up gas customers.* At the end of the first year, Holly and her mom packed up the fancy instant coffee her roommate had left behind and carried it back to their home in rural Pennsylvania, a good treat. All the way through college, her parents worried not about the money they spent for her room and board (because they didn't), but about the money that went to phone calls home and gas for the eight-hour roundtrip drive to shuttle her between college and home on breaks.

I thought about why it was so hard for Holly to pull away from her friends and attend to me. It was a big deal for her to be accepted by her graduate school friends mostly because she had long felt like an outsider. For her being able to finish her doctorate was a great measure of success, culturally and academically.

I now understand how she might have been frustrated that my presence was taking her away from her friends.

CHAPTER FIVE

Job Application

After arriving in Charlottesville, I found out that my visa alone didn't allow me to work. I had to apply for a work permit, which was going to take 365 dollars and three months to get. The first step in getting the work permit was to get my fingerprints taken, which meant we had to go to Charleston, West Virginia—a four-hour drive. Since we didn't want to go there the night before and spend the money on a hotel, we were left with no option but to leave Charlottesville at four in the morning. I had just landed in the country a week before, and picking me up from the airport had been a long drive for Holly. She wasn't excited about the idea of another long drive, but she also wanted me to be able to work and make money, so we drove there and came back the same day. It was a long and sometimes tense journey.

After the fingerprinting was done, waiting began. I would walk to the mailbox of our house every day to check whether my work permit had arrived. Everyone else in the house got mail and I would quickly sift through all of it but never see an envelope for me. I'd put the mail back in the box and start waiting for the next day.

In Lucknow, the local government and town planners had cut down most of the trees to make way for new buildings or roads. To be among trees, I had to go to the botanical gardens, an important landmark in my hometown, which were open to public for morning walks. I liked to go there every morning and enjoyed being surrounded by the greenery.

In Charlottesville, the entire city was like a botanical garden. I had arrived as autumn was beginning. The changing colors of leaves left me astounded. I often walked around the university with a camera in my hand. Every corner I turned, there was a tree asking to be photographed. I couldn't stop staring at trees that looked bright orange, or completely yellow, or just red.

Soon, I learned why the season was called fall in America. I had never seen trees shed leaves like this before. And then I learned a new verb: raking. The front yard of our house was filled with copious amounts of leaves. One day, while leaving the house for her class, Holly casually told me to "rake the leaves if you get bored." I didn't understand at first, but later found out that raking meant combing the yard with an instrument to get rid of the leaves.

With no money, no one that I could call, no one that I could share my feelings with, and no work permit, I had been feeling pretty worthless in America. I was angry with myself and in a desperate need to prove my worth, I decided to take my aggression out on the yard. I let out a few expletives in Hindi and grabbed the six-foot iron rod with a giant claw at one end, called a rake. I stood in the middle of the yard and began scraping the earth. I worked myself into frenzy. After several minutes of thrashing the leaves around, I hadn't made any progress. I had just moved the pile from one side to the other. The yard still looked like a big mess. My effort to clean it didn't make any difference. The mounds of leaves seemed like the big maze that was America. I was working with so much fervor that I didn't notice that I had bloodied my fingers in the process. I had turned my life upside down for a new beginning. I looked at my bleeding hand and wondered how much more I'd have to suffer.

December came. Now, there was not a single leaf on the trees and the grass looked lifeless. The days were so short that it got dark at five in the evening. I had been in the United States for almost three months. I was out of money and was still waiting for my work permit. Since it had gotten much colder, I had stopped walking up to the driveway to wait for the mailman. I mostly stayed inside my room, and looked for him through the window. Sometimes, I felt like the old and sad Indian mother in Indian movies who always waits for her lost son at the railway platform, hoping one day he will arrive. I felt sorry for myself.

On a cold afternoon in December, I found an envelope in the mailbox that said U.S. Immigration Services. It had my name peeking through the rectangular window. My heart was going a hundred miles an hour. My hands shook. I had been waiting for it so long that it seemed unreal that I was actually holding the letter. The letter seemed like a lottery ticket, a lottery that I wasn't sure that I'd won yet. I didn't think I had the nerve to open the letter.

I ran inside the house to show the letter to Holly. She looked at me, smiled, and took a deep breath as if to say, "Your wait seems to be over." She sliced the envelope open with a knife and pulled out a card the size of a credit card. It had my picture on the right side and "Employment Authorization Document" written on the top. I was elated. I didn't wait for it to get late enough in the morning for my parents to wake up in India. The work permit card felt like a key to a treasure, the solution to all my miseries.

I began applying for jobs. I wanted to work in radio, but there weren't enough paid jobs in the small town of Charlottesville. Some people suggested I move to Washington, DC to work for a public radio station, which I wasn't sure about since Holly had two years of coursework left. It didn't make a lot of sense to live away from Holly, when I had moved from halfway around the world to be with her. I started looking for jobs in Charlottesville. I tried my luck everywhere, but nothing worked. Every day that passed after I received my work permit seemed like a huge waste. I was missing out on making dollars, I thought.

Walking around town with Holly, I'd notice restaurants, bookstores, mattress stores, and jewelry stores displaying signs that said, "Now Hiring." I decided to apply for jobs at those shops. I had watched the employees and it didn't seem to me that the jobs required any special skill. It wouldn't be a bad idea to get some job, any job, while I continued to look for something better.

Thinking of applying for a sales job brought to mind a similar job that I had done a few years before in India. The work involved going door-to-door, knocking on people's homes and asking them to fill out a questionnaire, the objective being to persuade them to switch from their existing newspaper to the one I was working for. The job was humiliating. The pay was not great and it was demeaning to have people shut their doors in my face. I didn't tell any of my friends where I worked, and prayed that the door I knocked on didn't belong to someone I knew.

My parents and my close relatives had expected me to land a job with a fat salary, an air-conditioned office in the swank building of a multinational company. They were not going to be proud to hear that I was going around door-to-door selling a newspaper. I begged my boss to assign me an area of the city furthest away from where I lived, so I could avoid being seen by relatives and acquaintances. But soon my boss stopped paying attention to my requests and gave me locations I didn't want. Now, I had two options—either quit the job or find a way around knocking on people's doors. I chose the latter. I went to the area assigned to me, but didn't knock on doors. I just looked at the nameplates on the boundary walls and discreetly noted down each name and house number. When I got home, I filled out the questionnaire in the name of Mr. Gupta, Mr. Sharma, and Mr. Yadav. Since there was no pressure to convert people to our newspaper, I said the people were already our customers. It worked. My boss didn't pay much attention to the fact that the handwriting looked the same on every questionnaire. A month passed and I got my salary as I had every other month. The only difference was that this time I been paid for doing nothing.

I would soon find out that I was not the only person in the company who was doing this. My boss had been working there for a while and he'd had this happen to him before. It didn't occur to me that he could be double-checking, visiting or calling people's homes to find out whether I'd showed up at their place. I quit the job. I didn't want to have to answer to my boss.

Looking at the job advertisements in Charlottesville, I consoled myself that I was in America. Although it was a gigantic step down from what I had been doing in my last job, I was away from my family, who would have look down on me for working as a salesman. I filled out job applications in almost every store I came across. Most of them had a standard two-page form that had sections like "Work Experience," "Education," and "References." I didn't know why they couldn't just accept applicants' resumes instead of asking them to cram their entire life histories into two lines.

I spent several weeks applying and waiting to be called for an interview. "Sorry, we found someone who had more relevant experience," would be the answer when I called the employer to check whether they were interested in my application. People didn't want to interview me because I didn't have any experience in retail, and they didn't care that I had a master's degree in business. My last job in India had spoilt me, and had turned me to into an overconfident, arrogant man. I couldn't imagine any of these jobs I was applying for in the United States being too difficult. After all, they only required a high school diploma, I thought. I got the feeling that my resume didn't look familiar to most hiring managers, so they buried it at the bottom of the pile. They were probably looking for a familiar name—Robert, Dan, Keith—and my name didn't quite click. My work experience, references, and educational institutions looked too alien. There were no columns on the job applications to describe my confidence, enthusiasm, sense of humor, or eagerness to work.

I believed that if I could sit in front of a person and get a chance to talk one-on-one, I could convince someone to give me the job. I looked for the number of ElectronicsHut, an electronics chain store where I had applied for a job. Someone called Mike answered the phone and said, "How can I help you?"

"I have applied for the position of sales associate in your store and was wondering whether I could get an interview," I said nervously.

"Hang on a second. What's your name?"

"Deepak."

"The book?"

"No, no, no, it's D-e-e-p-a-k. Deepak Singh." I pronounced each consonant and vowel as clearly as I could.

"Oh, okay, let me check."

I heard papers rustling in the background.

"Alright, I found your application. Could you come for an interview on Monday at 10 A.M.?"

CHAPTER SIX

Hired

Monday came. I wore a white shirt and a pair of grey pants and got on bus number 7. Almost every seat was taken. The bus seemed to be a labor carrier, especially at that time of the morning. It picked up people with vacant faces and lunchboxes and water bottles from various locations of the city, places that I hadn't seen before. At nine in the morning, they seemed to be saying, "Is it five yet?"

The bus reminded me of the large pickup trucks that brought unskilled workers from the neighboring villages to the city of Lucknow every morning. The vulnerable day laborers got off close to the coffee house, an important landmark in the city. They massed across the street to make themselves available to the city folks.

I remembered going to the city center to pick up a handful of workers in order to get my house painted or to get some other repair done. As I'd approach them, they'd surround me, desperate, two inches from face, begging to get hired. When I noticed someone looking especially miserable, I'd use that to exploit the wage. I would choose the one who agreed to work the most number of hours for the least amount of money. After being in the United States for a while, I hated myself for having done that.

On bus number 7, I was the one who was going to beg to be hired, I was the one who was vulnerable, I was the one who was going to be exploited.

I showed up at the store and after I had stood around for a few minutes, someone came up to me.

"What can I help you find?"

"I am here for an interview."

"Oh, let me go get Mike." He returned shortly and said, "He'll be right out."

A couple of minutes later, a middle-aged, pot-bellied, crew-cut, white man of average height came out with a blue clipboard in his hand.

"Hi, I'm Mike," he said. "How are ya?" He extended his hand to shake mine.

"Fine, thanks. How are you?"

"Hungry! Haven't eaten since morning. This is what you get for being in the retail business," he said with a grin. I looked at him and thought about what he meant. Why did retail stop him from eating?

"Sorry you had to wait. Come on in," he gestured for me to follow him.

He took me into a room full of large cardboard boxes, piled up to the ceiling on movable racks. Other boxes were crowded on the floor, stuffed with alarm clocks, batteries, wires, and other kinds of gadgets. A white computer table and a black swivel chair were tucked in a corner. Above the computer, on the desk, was a shelf that had a printer, several cables running in different directions, and a very small television that kept changing images every three seconds.

He climbed over the stuff spilling out of the boxes on the floor, and pulled out a chair. "Have a seat," he said, and sat down on a step stool. As I looked around the room, he said, "Yeah, I know, but trust me, it's not this messy all the time. I'm in the middle of putting up merchandise." I gave him a smile and fixed my shirt collar for the interview.

He looked through my resume. "So, you've never worked in retail before, hmmm." He looked up with a concerned face and said, "Do you know something about electronics?"

I answered, "I like them and I am sure I will learn more about them once I get to use them."

He gave me a warm smile, and asked, "Can you hook up a wall phone?"

I wasn't sure how a wall phone was different from any other phone, and what he meant by *hooking it up*. I wanted to say yes, but at the same time I didn't want him to hand me a wall phone to demonstrate. I said, "I should be able to."

He nodded his head in a slow motion and rubbed his index finger on his lower lip as if he didn't believe me. His body language was not making me feel comfortable, but I was still confident that I could do the job. How hard could it be to sell a gadget, I thought? The customer walks in and asks for whatever he wants and the salesman hands him the product and takes his money—as simple as that.

He asked me some general questions about my integrity—what would I do if I saw an employee stealing, and had I ever stolen from my previous employers? After a few minutes of going through his notes, he flicked the clip on the clipboard with his thumb, and said, "Congratulations, you are hired. You will work at a different branch of this store."

I asked, "What's the salary like?"

"Well, this is not a salaried job. You get paid by the hour here, but if you work your way up and become a manager, you get a salary."

"What's the hourly pay?" I said.

"It can range anywhere between seven and fifteen bucks an hour. Depends how hard you work and how good a salesman you are."

I had never worked on an hourly basis before, and I didn't understand what he meant.

"When can I start?"

He said, "Your manager, Cindy, will give you a call and let you know." He shook my hand, and gave me a white packet. "Here's some reading material for ya."

I left his office feeling happy that I had been successful in my first interview in America, although it was not the job of my choice. A couple of days later a very authoritative-sounding woman called my house and said, "Hi, this is Cindy. Is this Deepak?"

"Yes, it's him."

"I was calling to tell you that we are waiting for your background check. I will call you when I have your information and then you can start. In most cases it takes just under a week. But I am not sure how long it will be in your case, since it has to go through India."

I told her I was anxious to work and would wait for her call. "Well, you're gonna have to wait for the background check. I can't let you start before that, alright?" I heard the sound of the phone receiver hitting the base as soon as I said okay. Once again, I started waiting. I felt helpless; it seemed like I had spent the last three months in America waiting—waiting to get my work permit, waiting to get better after falling sick, waiting for people to give me a job interview, and now waiting for this background check.

I called the store after a week. The woman who answered the phone said, "I don't see anything on my fax machine. I will call you when I get your papers." I waited for another week and called again to get the same answer. Cindy's tone became less friendly every time I called.

Since I had never committed any crime, I started wondering why it was taking so long to get my background checked. After about five weeks, I got a call from the district office of the company. Someone named Lindsay called and said, "Is Deepak there?"

I had to ask her to repeat herself at least three times before I could make out that she was saying, "Is Deepak there?" She was from West Virginia with a mountain accent and pronounced *there* as *theyur*. When I said she was speaking to Deepak, she said, "Listen, I've been calling at your work in India but no one seems to be there."

"What time do you call?" I asked.

"I call between eleven and three during the day." I immediately knew why my store manager hadn't received my background check papers. I tried to explain, "Lindsay, there is a ten-hour difference between India and the United States, people are sleeping when you call there."

"Oh, really?" she exclaimed. Her tone reminded me of a time when I had told an illiterate farmer in India that a man had landed on the moon. He was just as surprised. After a few moments of awkward silence on the phone, Lindsay said, "Can you provide a local reference?"

"Yes," I said and gave her a phone number of a local contact.

A couple of hours later, Cindy called and said I could start working the next day. I wondered why it took Lindsay so long to realize that there might be a reason why people in India weren't answering her calls. I also wondered if the doorman there—who guarded the office by staying awake the whole night—ever thought it was eerie that the phone rang in the early hours of the morning, every day, for a whole month.

The next day I presented myself at the store, dressed in a light-blue button-down shirt and khakis. According to the manual that I had received after my interview with Mike, employees could only wear light-colored plain shirts and dark pants. The last time I had worn a uniform was in high school.

It was ten in the morning and the store had just opened. Cindy—I recognized her voice—was helping a customer. I stood in the television section and stared at one of the big screens on the wall. A few minutes later, Cindy walked up to me and said, "Hi, what can I help you find today, sir?"

"My name is Deepak, and I am looking for Cindy."

"Oh, hi, Deepak," she said and burst into loud laughter. "I am Cindy, I thought you were a customer." She continued laughing. I smiled, and wondered what was so funny. "Alright, come on in."

She took me to a backroom that looked neat and orderly—quite different from Mike's. She gave me a black swivel chair to sit in and sat herself down on a similar looking seat.

She started flipping through some papers in a cream-colored folder. "Awright," she said and pulled out what looked like my resume, "since I didn't interview you, let me quickly go through your application and see what you've done before."

"Okay," I said. I noticed her eyes doing a run-through of my resume.

"Awrighty." She put it back in the folder and said, "I'm gonna give you a form to fill out your available hours and days of the week."

I looked at the sheet she handed me. It had several rows and columns, rows for days of the week and columns for hours of the day. I checked myself available for every hour and day the store was open. I handed back the sheet and she said, "Do you have any questions?"

"Yes, I do, actually," I said.

"Go ahead."

"Could you please explain the pay structure? I didn't understand it very well in my interview."

"Sure, it's minimum wage plus commission," she said. She pointed towards an employee. "That's Jackie. She makes about twelve bucks an hour." She looked at me and smiled and said, "So if you can sell like her you can make as much as her or more, there's no limit."

She smiled at me again, and pointed towards a different employee and said in a hushed voice, "That's Ron, and he doesn't make more than seven bucks an hour. You know why?" I didn't know why, but I made a guess and said, "He is not as good a salesman."

"Exactly, and he is on his way out," she said and smiled in a way that gave me the impression that she was trying to drive the point home to me. There was something strange about her smile; I couldn't tell if she was in a good mood and being nice to me, or if she was angry. She spoke with a sharp and commanding voice.

"May I ask," I swallowed and said, "another question?"

She said, "Of course!"

"Since, this job is so much about selling, will I get some training?"

"Oh, yes. You will spend your entire first week sitting in this chair taking certifications online." She turned around and put her hand on a desktop computer. "The company is very strict about training; we don't let our employees go on the sales floor until they are confident about the products we sell."

"Okay," I said and took a deep breath. I was already feeling overwhelmed by the pressure to perform, the number of things to learn, and the need to build a rapport with my coworkers and, most importantly, with my boss. I wondered if there was a training manual for an Indian coming to work for the first time in America.

Cindy rose from her chair and said, "Let me first give you a tour of the store and introduce you to the employees." She walked out of the backroom into the main part of the store, and I followed. She started from the entrance and pointed towards a wall and said, "This is our cell phone wall. We sell prepaid phones and contract phones and carry products from three different companies."

She moved on to the next section while I listened carefully. "This is our home entertainment section. We sell small boom boxes and home theater systems." We shifted to another part of the store and she pointed to some products that looked like long, thin antennas, like the ones installed on trucks.

"This is where we keep radio scanners, radar detectors, and CB radios." She spent less than fifteen minutes walking me around the store and pointing at what seemed like fifteen hundred products—many of which I hadn't seen or heard of before.

Then she introduced me to Ron, an overweight, middle-aged, light-skinned, half-bald, African American man with a goatee. Ron was carrying a box full of wires and batteries. He put the box down, shook my hand, and said, "Hi, nice to meetcha." His voice was deep and hoarse. He wore a well-ironed navy-blue shirt that had three pens clipped on its pocket.

"Nice to meet you, too," I said and smiled at him, but Ron didn't smile back. He picked up his box and walked away.

Cindy gestured for the other employee to come to us. "Jackie, this is our new employee, Deepak. Deepak, this is Jackie. She's been here the longest." Jackie was a young-looking African American woman who was quick to shake my hand. She gave me a big friendly smile. I returned the smile and said, "Nice to meet you, Jackie."

Although everyone seemed cordial, I got the feeling that they were trying to glance at me when I was not looking. I had had that happen at my previous jobs in India too—people trying to check out the new employee, his behavior, mannerisms, style of dressing. I didn't have anything in common with Cindy, Ron, or Jackie. There were strange vibes between us. I had to learn to speak like them, to understand the jobs they did, to coexist and be friends. I had to learn a whole lot more than any other American who just wanted to get a job in retail.

"Come on back, Deepak!" said Cindy as she started walking towards the backroom. "Let me set you up on this computer so you can start taking your certifications." She logged me onto the company's website and said, "Here you go, you're all set." She got up from her chair and gestured with her hands for me to sit down.

I smiled and took the chair. She said, "I'll be out front. If you got any questions, come get me, awright?"

I started reading and answering questions about various electronics—satellite radios, wireless home security systems, digital weather thermometers, digital answering machines, digital baby monitors, digital shower radios, digital metal detectors, digital radio scanners, digital this and digital that. There was a lot to know, and so much to remember. As I read about the products and their uses, I wondered why people in America wanted to listen to the radio while they showered, why they wanted to find buried pieces of metal in their backyards, why they left their infants and babies in another room and then monitored them with the help of electronic gadgets, why they wanted to listen to conversations between police officers or firefighters on their radio scanners.

Cindy walked in while I was staring at the computer screen, puzzled with all these thoughts. "Deepak, you got any questions?"

I looked at her, smiled, took a deep breath, and said, "I am okay, thanks!"

After a week of sitting in the backroom and going through hundreds of products, their features, technical specifications, and accessories, I was formally done with the training. When I finished my last module, a message popped up on the computer screen: *Congrats! Now you are ready to answer any questions that your customers may ask.* It felt good to see that, but I wasn't sure if I was ready to tackle the customers.

It wasn't that difficult to read about the products on the computer and answer questions by picking an answer out of five possible choices. I had the uneasy feeling that customers were not going to offer me multiple-choice questions.

CHAPTER SEVEN

First Day

I had been on the sales floor for only a few minutes when I saw a middle-aged Indian couple walking in. My heart jumped. I took off my nametag, out of impulse, and slipped it into my shirt pocket. I tried to not be the first one to talk to them, and I pretended to look like a shopper myself. I was embarrassed to be talking to another Indian as a salesman.

I saw my parents in the bespectacled, grey-haired man and the fifty-year-old woman. I couldn't look in their eyes when they looked at me. I went to hide in the backroom.

Then Cindy came into the backroom and said, "Deepak, we have some Indian shoppers who want to buy a DVD player and they want to know if it would work in India. I told them one of our team members is from India. He can answer your question better than anyone else," she said, with a grin on her face.

I had to come out.

The man smiled at me, and said, "Are you from India?"

"Yes, I am," I said and smiled back.

"Which part?"

"North. I am from Lucknow."

"Okay. We are from Mumbai."

"You have a question?" I asked.

"Yes, yes. My son is in medical school here. We were visiting him, but now we are going back," the lady said and scanned me top to bottom.

"Okay, what can I help you with?" I said, trying to avoid the next question. Back in India, mothers of my friends often volunteered their son's salary and then quickly asked mine. It was their way of judging their son's success.

"We are trying to buy a DVD player, but we want to make sure that it will work in India."

"Let me see," I said, and walked to DVD section.

"Are you also studying at the university?" the man asked.

"No, I am not."

"So, what are you doing here?" he said with a curious face.

"I am working here," I said.

He fired the next question. "What's your background?"

"Yes, this DVD will work in India," I said.

"Okay, good."

"And my background is in media," I said. "I am in new in America and I am trying to find a better job."

"Yes, I was thinking about that. You seemed to be an educated chap. You can do better than this," the man replied. I don't know why, but I was acting as if the couple would fly to India, and go straight to Lucknow and tell my parents about what was I doing. Out of more than one billion Indians in India and around the world, the chances of the Indian shopper in my store turning out to be someone who knew my parents were next to zero. But it didn't matter. I couldn't get the inhibition out of my system.

When the training finished, I had no business being in the backroom unless I was unboxing the newly arrived merchandise. All of a sudden I was in the open. My first reaction was to avoid being seen working as a salesman by anyone who looked to be Indian.

Although I didn't know any of the Indians who came to shop, it seemed as if I could read their minds when they saw me working at the store. "You pathetic loser," they seemed to say. "You came to America to do this?"

I took a deep breath after the Indian couple left. In the next few minutes a white lady came into the store. She looked to be in her eighties and walked very slowly. Cindy gestured for me to take the initiative and help her. I waited until she came up to the counter where I was standing. I didn't say anything. She came up to me and said, "Hi, I am looking for a battery for my watch."

My brain did a quick search through all knowledge about batteries that I had acquired a few days ago. She took her wristwatch off and set it on the counter; I found myself clueless. I knew that I had learned about finding batteries for watches, but I couldn't recall anything. I asked her, "Do you know what kind of battery this watch takes?"

"I don't know, but you guys should be able to look it up on your computer, can't you?" I looked at Ron, who was dusting some merchandise.

"Hey, Ron, could you please help me?" I said.

He stopped dusting and came up to the counter, picked up the customer's watch, put it back down, turned around, grabbed a battery pack, handed it to me, and walked away without saying anything.

The customer looked at Ron with a smile and said, "That was easy!"

"It comes from years of experience and a lot of knowledge," Ron said.

"Well, you made it look real easy. It seemed you could tell by just looking at the watch what kind of battery it required."

"Yep, knowledge and experience, that's what it is." Ron laughed in self-appreciation.

I put my password into the register, and scanned the barcode on the battery pack. I told the lady her total was three dollars and twenty-nine cents. She opened her purse and started looking for something. She said, "Oh, there it is," and pulled out a checkbook.

She set the book on the counter, fixed her glasses, brought her head very close to be able to see clearly, and started writing a check for three dollars and twenty-nine cents. While her pen moved slowly on the paper, I started wondering about the steps involved in accepting money in the form of a check.

I asked for Ron's help again. He replied with a sigh. He came with heavy steps, and asked the lady to show some kind of ID. When she presented her driver's license, he hit a key on the keyboard, and started entering details from her license onto the computer.

I watched Ron go through several steps—noting down the customer's identification details, stamping the back of the check with red ink, and keeping the check in a special drawer—all for just three dollars and twenty-nine cents.

When Ron was entering details from her driver's license, I noticed the date of birth of the customer. She was born in 1926. It was the same year my grandfather was born. I was quite attached to him. He died when I was only seven years of age, but I could never forget his date of birth. I couldn't help but tell the lady that my grandfather was born in the same year she had, and that he had been dead for more than twenty-five years.

Putting the driver's license back in her purse with shaking hands, she said, "Well, I am still here." She smiled, turned around, and walked out slowly.

As I watched her leave the store, I wondered if she had any children, or grandchildren, and felt sorry for her that in her old age she had to come and buy a watch battery herself. My grandmother, who died at the age of eighty, often asked me to get her eyeglasses fixed, pick up her medicines, or mail letters; she never had to go anywhere herself. I couldn't imagine her going to buy a watch battery on her own. People would have judged my family very harshly if she had to do that. I am sure my neighbors and friends would have thought we were selfish and irresponsible.

While I was lost in these thoughts about my first customer, Cindy put down the screwdriver she was using to tighten a shelf on the TV wall, and walked hastily towards me.

She came up to me, brought her face right up to mine, and stared at me from only a few inches away—all I could see was her white face. Smiling, but with gritted teeth, she said, "Awright, what did you learn about customer service in your training?" I stood there blankly, and said nothing. She said, "Let me remind you and don't you ever forget that every customer has to be greeted within five seconds of setting foot in this store, awright?"

I said, "I will not forget this."

She stepped back, pointed towards the entrance, and said, "Also, you should walk up to the customer, and not wait for him to come up to you." When I said okay, she raised her one thumb up in the air, and said, "Awright!" She smiled again and went back to what she was doing.

I'd forgotten to greet the customer, and I had waited for her to come to me, because I wasn't confident that I'd be able to answer her questions. Things got quiet after Cindy's rant. I felt awkward. I didn't know if this was how American bosses talked to their workers, or if it was just Cindy. While these thoughts filled my head, I decided to defuse the awkwardness, and asked Jackie to show me how to find a battery. I wanted to learn it myself so that I didn't have to ask someone every time a customer came looking for something.

Jackie was enthusiastic and keen to teach me. She hit a red button on the keyboard that said "Hot." It took us to the company's webpage. She clicked on the menu and selected a tab that said "Batteries."

"Now," she said, "you have to put in the model number of the watch and it will tell you which battery you need. Easy, ain't it?" She looked at me and smiled. Jackie made me feel better. Her smile was reassuring. She told me she would help with other things, but she was getting off work soon that day.

While I pondered this, I saw two young ladies coming in with a plastic bag in their hands. They walked straight up to me.

"Hi, how can I help you?" I said.

"We just wanna make a return," one of them said.

I took them to the cash register. They pulled an alarm clock out of the bag and set it on the counter. This was the first return of the day, and the only thing I could remember from the training was that it was a lengthy procedure. It was easy if the money was to be refunded to a credit card, but if the purchase had been made with a check, I was required to feed a lot of data into the computer and ask the customer many questions.

The procedure became even more of an ordeal if the purchase had been made more than thirty days ago, or if the customer was trying to return the merchandise without a receipt. Since I was going to be doing this for the first time, I wanted to get it right. I told the customers that I was still in training, and I needed to ask my colleague—who was helping another customer at that moment—for his help.

By the time Ron returned ten minutes later, the ladies' patience had reached its limit. They were tapping their fingers on the counter, making me nervous. I realized it would take much longer if I did it myself while Ron watched me. So I said, "Ron, could you please help these ladies?"

But, contrary to what I was hoping, Ron said, "Why don't you do it yourself—I'll watch you."

I felt cold sweat on my forehead. I dreaded beginning the process, but I had no choice. I was the one who had originally talked to these women, so they were my customers. There was no one else in the store who could help me. I had two angry women staring at me from the other side of the counter, and Ron watching me struggle.

I began entering the information from the receipt into the computer, pushing one key at a time, with my chin digging into my chest, trying not to look at the customers in front of me, and turning to Ron for his help at every step. I asked the customer, "What's your zip code?" Irked at my slow speed, she said, "It should be there on the receipt." I looked down carefully and found it at the very bottom. I noticed Ron and the customers exchanging a sarcastic smile.

"How long have you been working here?" one of the customers asked me in a sharp tone.

"This is my first day," I replied.

"You've been training for a week," Ron said, "You should know how to do this." He looked at the ladies, and gave the ladies an exasperated eye roll. I looked at him, surprised. I wasn't expecting him to say that in front of a customer.

I printed out the return receipt and handed it to the ladies. They looked at me, smiled, and one of them said, "You'll get there." As I saw them walking out of the store, I took a deep breath and wiped the sweat off my forehead. I felt like I had just endured the longest twenty minutes of my life. I thought Ron could have helped me not to lose face in front of the customers, but instead he had watched me go through the humiliation.

I looked at my watch and said, "It is almost time to go."

"Not yet," Ron said. "We gotta do a few things before we close. Why don't you grab the vacuum cleaner and I'll count the money in the cash register."

I wondered if Ron hadn't tried to help me because he was insecure and not a good enough salesman himself. I wasn't sure.

I left work after a very long and emotionally exhausting day. Holly came to pick me up, since the city buses stopped running after nine at night. After I put on the seatbelt, she put the car in gear, and we drove off.

A few seconds later she asked me, "So, how was your first day on the sales floor?" I didn't know where to begin. I wasn't sure if the eighty-five-year-old lady coming to get a watch battery was more shocking than Cindy berating me for bad customer service, or if not being able to help the two young women was more embarrassing.

Holly looked at me after I didn't respond, and said, "How was your day, honey?" I took a deep breath. She said, "It's alright, we can talk when we get home."

CHAPTER EIGHT

One Month's Notice

The next morning, the bus dropped me off at the mall a few minutes before the stores were supposed to open. The weekend was still a few days away, and the mall was empty—except for an elderly couple, both wearing sneakers, who walked speedily without paying any attention to the half-naked mannequins peeking at them through the glass windows of the Victoria's Secret, or to the glittering diamond rings in Zales.

As they walked by, the man said, "Opening a little early today, Brittany?" to a lanky white girl who revealed a large green tattoo on her lower back as she bent down to lift the shutters of the Auntie Anne's pretzel shop. Brittany replied, "Yeah, gotta start early today."

The couple waved a hello to a massively overweight, bearded black man who pushed the cart equipped with cleaning supplies. The janitor stopped at each store and looked at the objects in the window for a few minutes before he moved to the next one. The husband and the wife seemed to be regular walkers in the mall—they passed me three times while I strolled aimlessly, and waited for it to be time to go to work.

As I walked past a cell phone accessories kiosk across from Ritz Camera, I noticed a dark-haired head in the midst of the hanging faceplates and carrying cases for wireless phones. I slowed down to take a look. The lady looked to be Indian, and she said, "Can I help you?" I was happily surprised to see her, and hear her familiar accent. I tried to hide my excitement, but instead of responding to her question, I asked where she was from. She responded, "India, what can I help you with today?"

I was expecting that she would ask me if I was from India too, and then I would ask what part of India she came from, and then maybe we could talk in Hindi. She looked straight into my eyes, waiting to know if I was interested in buying anything she sold. I didn't get a friendly vibe from her, so I said, apologetically, "Sorry to bother you, but I got excited to see another Indian in the mall."

She smiled, "Oh, no problem, my husband is running late this morning, and I am trying to open the kiosk on my own."

"I understand. I work in an electronics store a few shops down. I'll come another time." I looked at my wristwatch and saw it was almost time for my store to open.

I walked quickly and saw that the glass front door of my store was shut, but the lights inside were on and the backroom door was half opened. I pushed the glass door to see if it had been unlocked; it had. As I walked in I could hear the Black Eyed Peas pouring out of the demo satellite radio. Cindy was sitting at her desk in the backroom with a large Starbucks cup. She was straining her eyes to look at the computer screen, working the mouse with her right hand, and holding what seemed like last night's sales receipts in her left.

When I said hello, she shook her head as if she were waking up from a dream. "Oh, you scared me, I didn't know you were here," she said and laughed. "Let me know if you get busy on the floor. Jackie is running late by an hour this morning."

Soon, a white-haired man sauntered into the store. As he came close, I noticed that his eyebrows were white too. I asked if I could help him.

"Yeah, I'm lookin' for a shower radio."

I knew we carried shower radios, but I'd never had a customer come in to buy one. Among the variety of electronics that we carried in the store, the shower radio was the most intriguing to me. I always wondered what they were for. The name was self-explanatory, but why there had to be a radio in a shower, I didn't understand. In my mind, the two things had nothing to do with each other. When you were listening to the radio, you wouldn't be taking a shower, and when you were taking a shower, why would you want to listen to the radio? The product was under ten dollars and since it was not the most popular item, I had never bothered to learn more about it. When this man in the store said he was looking for one, it brought to mind the same questions again.

"You got one?" said the man.

"Yes, we do have those. Let me grab one for you."

He was about my height. Old age seemed to have curved his spine. He talked with his hands behind his back. I brought out a shower radio and gave it to him.

"Thank you, young man," he said. Wrinkles bunched up around his eyes as he smiled. He had a pleasant manner about him. Since he was the only customer in the store, I asked him, "Do you mind telling me what you are going to do with this radio?"

"Ah, my wife gets pissed when I listen to the radio when she's around. I can't hear very well so I have to keep the volume cranked up pretty high. She hates that." I smiled. "I thought maybe I could get a shower radio. I'm an old man and I spend a lot of time in the bathroom. I could listen to it there."

In India, our family of five shared one bathroom. The five-square-foot space in our apartment was prime real estate at eight in the morning. Also, we didn't have an endless water supply. We got water for two hours in the morning and two hours in the evening. With one bathroom between five people and limited water supply, there was barely enough time for all of us to defecate, brush, shave, and shower. There was no time for listening to the radio. If my father spent more than five minutes there, everyone else knocked on the door until he got out. If I took a little longer, my brother hurled abuses from outside the door.

I looked at the old man said, "How old are you, sir?"

"Well, let's put it this way. I've had more surgeries on my body than your age," he said and laughed. He looked old, but he acted young and happy. I waited for him to tell me his age. "I am eighty." I didn't think he was that old. I was guessing seventy.

"You look good for your age," I said.

"I am okay, but I can't pee very well. Spend too much time in the john. That's why the radio." I enjoyed talking with him. He bought the radio and thanked me for helping him.

After a few minutes, a young white man walked in. I greeted him and walked toward him to offer help. He took a detour around a shelf, and went straight to the cell phone wall at the very back of the store. It seemed like he knew what he wanted and didn't want any help. Cindy came out and pointed at me and then at the guy with her index finger. I got the message from reading her lips, "Help him!" She must have seen the guy on the backroom TV, which was hooked up to the store camera.

I made a second attempt at the customer and asked if he needed any help. He said, "Yes, I'm looking for a cell phone, but I'm not sure which service provider I should sign up with." I knew from my training that selling cell phones was a good way of making commissions. I had also learned a lot of information in training about selling them. Now that this customer was standing in front of me asking for my advice, all the details became a blur in my mind.

As much as I wanted to help him and to make a sale, I didn't know what to say or where to start. I stood there in silence looking at the cell phone wall, pretending I was trying to think which service would be good for him. The customer waited, as if he appreciated that I was taking my time to come up with the right answer.

When the pause became too long and got awkward, I said, "I'm sorry, I am not from this area, but my manager will be able to help you. Let me go and get her." The customer smiled as if to say, "That's totally fine!"

I quickly stepped away and asked Cindy, "Could you help me make a cell phone sale?" She smiled and said, "I'd be more than happy to." She took a final swig from the Starbucks cup, and threw it in the trashcan next to her chair. She put on a happy face to greet the customer. "Sir, what can I help you with today?"

"Umm, yeah I was looking for a cell phone that works in this area."

"Okay, are you gonna be living in Charlottesville mostly, or will you be moving around a lot?"

"I'll be in Charlottesville most of the time."

I was watching Cindy carefully and paying attention to what questions she asked the customer. There was a lot of genuine enthusiasm in her voice. The sale was made in no time. She then went around the store picking different accessories for the cell phone, and laid them on the counter. The guy didn't seem sure, and asked if he really needed the carrying case.

She replied, "Oh, yeah, you don't want your two-hundred-dollar phone to drop and break by accident." She threw her own phone on the floor to demonstrate the utility of the case. Cindy had good aim—the phone rolled down and landed near his feet. He picked it up and looked at it.

"Sure, why not. I'll get it." A sales gimmick, I thought, but it worked. The man, who had walked into the store twenty minutes ago looking for a cell phone, walked out with a bag full of products he hadn't known he wanted.

A few more days passed. Although I had learned a good number of things, I often found myself clueless when trying to answer questions from the customers. In order to avoid embarrassment, I came up with excuses like, "I am new," "I am still training," and, "Today is my sixth day—or eighth day."

Some of the customers were nice and waited until I figured out what they wanted, and some of them were not so nice. It shook my confidence. I dreaded going to work on busy days, mostly weekends, when the store would be filled with customers, and Jackie, Cindy, and Ron were all on the sales floor helping customers and had no time to answer my questions.

I'd be stuck with tricky questions. "Y'all program radio scanners?" "I live in Scottsville and I don't get no reception on my cell phone. Y'know what service works in my area?" "I'm a truck driver and I'm lookin' for an antenna for my CB radio, y'all have 'em?" "I'm trynna come outta a quarter-inch jack of an audio receiver, goin' into a one-eighth-inch jack of an MP3 player—you got that kinda cable?" Not able to understand what they were talking about, I'd look at them with an empty expression as if they were speaking another language, which, in a way, they were. I would have to wait for one of my colleagues to help me decipher where the customer was coming from and where he wanted to go, what worked in Scottsville, and what CB radio antenna would be best for him.

It frustrated me that I had to rely on other people for every other question. Sometimes, Cindy would get irritated, point towards the computer, and say, "Look it up on the company's website, you'll find it." But computers only understand the specific name of a product, not a convoluted phrase like, "I am trynna to come outta." I would continue to wait for someone to help me.

It got to the point where I started hiding from the customers. If I saw someone walking into the store, my first reaction would be to walk in the opposite direction, bend down under the counter, or hide behind a shelf pretending I was looking for something or dusting the merchandise.

I desperately hoped that someone else would take care of the customer. My two college degrees—with concentrations in sales, marketing, human resource management, and consumer behavior—hadn't taught me anything about working sales in America. This brought to mind my friend in India who worked in a call center. His job was to call Americans and remind them to pay their credit card bills. He often complained about not being able to understand their accents and having trouble making himself understood. Although he had gone through several weeks of voice and accent training, he still complained about Americans yelling at him. Now I could relate to what he was going through, since I had trouble talking with them even when I was there in person.

One time, the district manager paid a surprise visit to our store. Cindy wasn't prepared for it. She panicked, and started saying to every employee in a hushed voice, "Offer every customer accessories, awright?" "Greet the customers!" "Don't forget to wear your badges!" I had never seen her so scared. The district manager stood in one corner of the store and watched everyone. Cindy, Ron, and Jackie all seemed to be extra courteous to the customers, saying hellos, welcomes, and thank-yous more enthusiastically than ever before. Watching everyone act differently, I started doing the same thing, but also I didn't want to be caught not being able to answer a customer's question.

I saw a tall white man taking long strides into the store towards me. The chances of me being able to answer his question were fifty-fifty. If he asked for something simple, like batteries, a digital camera, a portable radio, or an alarm clock, I could just grab it from the backroom, but if he had a question that involved hooking up two devices, programming a cell phone, or something of an equally complicated nature, I would be clueless.

I didn't want to have to ask for help from other employees on a day when the district manager was visiting. That would have been a surefire way of getting fired. I walked away from the customer and heard someone else greet him. He had only came in to ask how late we were open. The district manager was quick to notice what I had done.

He gestured at me with his index finger to follow him outside the store's front door, and gestured for Cindy to come out too. When she came, he asked me, "What's your name?"

"Deepak," I said.

"What are you supposed to do when a customer walks into your store?" He was a tall, middle-aged white man in a suit and tie, with a leather bag in his right hand.

It took me a while before I could utter any words. Cindy looked at me in the way a parent looks at a child to encourage him to recite the poem to the guests.

I forced out a sentence, "Greet him, and then ask him how we could help him."

"Exactly. Then why did you start walking away from him? *Why?*" I didn't say anything. "Do you have an answer?" I kept quiet, because I didn't have an answer. I noticed Cindy tapping fingers on her thigh, looking in a different direction. "Can I get your word that this won't happen again?"

"Yes," I said. He shook my hand firmly, and smiled. I walked back onto the floor and prayed to God that he'd leave soon. When he had gone, Cindy called everyone for a quick meeting. She said, "Listen, guys, I want to make this clear to you all: if my ass is gonna be chewed, be sure that I will chew yours."

She paused for a second and looked everyone in the eye, one after the other. "You know what I mean?" Everyone nodded. She continued, "The DM gave me a real hard time about the sales numbers—we are not making it. The goal for last month was thirty thousand dollars, and we didn't even get close to that figure." She paused to reveal her gritted teeth. "And the customer service was pathetic today." She turned to me and rested her gaze on my face until I got fidgety. She said, "Deepak, I am gonna have to put you on a month's notice."

Silence followed after she said that. Jackie and Ron looked grim. I could tell that this was bad news for me, but wasn't sure how bad. "What does that mean?" I asked. She replied, "It means if your sales numbers don't improve by next month, I will have to let you go." I didn't say anything. "I'm sorry, but I have been sent to this store only a month ago, and my job is to straighten things out here," she said. "The last manager was an asshole, and he is the reason why no one comes to shop in this store."

She looked at everyone and smiled. "I can't do this without the help of my employees." She asked, "Are you guys gonna help me?"

Jackie raised a fist and said, "Yesss!"

Ron said, "I always help everybody."

She looked at me and said, "Deepak, you've got a month to prove yourself."

I had never been given any kind of warning at my jobs in India. None of my bosses had thought I wasn't capable, or that I was not able to perform. Getting a month's notice from Cindy reminded me of a being in seventh grade, and flunking math and two science subjects in my half-yearly exams. My class teacher had written in my homework diary, "Poor performance. Parents must come and meet the subject teachers." She asked me to bring the diary back with my parents' signatures on the note. I dreaded showing it to my mother.

I often did poorly in math, but actually not being able to get passing grades was a matter of serious concern. Most parents thought there were only two respectable professions to pursue—medicine or engineering—and not doing well in math and biology meant that I was a hopeless student. After a few days in which I avoided looking into my teacher's eyes, she warned me again to bring my parents to the school. I finally presented my exam results to my mother. She was rolling dough to make *chapatis*. She looked at my grades marked in red ink and didn't say anything. I looked at her then looked down as if I had committed an unforgivable crime. I noticed her gazing at the ceiling with her head resting on the kitchen wall. It seemed like she was trying to think what would become of me if I couldn't become a doctor or an engineer.

She came to the school the next day and the teacher told her in front of the whole class that if I didn't do well in my final exams, I would have to repeat the year in seventh grade. We walked out of the classroom, and my mother didn't say anything to me. Generally, she yelled at me if I did anything she didn't like, but her silence made it obvious that I had disappointed her so deeply that it wasn't worth her while to scold me. Her silence was a far stronger chastisement. When Cindy told me that I only had a month to prove myself, the task ahead felt equally hard.

CHAPTER NINE

English

I wanted to talk with Ron and get to know him, but he didn't seem to care. One evening we were working together, and after a few awkward moments of silence, I said, "How long have you been working here?"

"Three months in this store, but I have a lot of sales experience."

"What did you do before this?"

"Lots of things, I don't even know where to start." I waited for him to say more. "I was in the military for a while, and traveled to a lot of places around the world."

"Have you been to India?"

"Oh, no. I don't trust the Middle East." I didn't understand why he had brought up the Middle East. Before I could tell him India was in South Asia, not the Middle East, he said, "I got two diplomas and several certifications and I am training to be a manager." I nodded. He was the oldest worker in the store and talked like he knew what he was talking about. I asked him for some advice.

"What do you think I should do in order to do well in this job?"

Ron made a study of me.

"See, the problem witchu is that you don't speak English. So, first of all, you need to learn the language to survive in America. Then everything depends on you. If you wanna do well, you can do it, but it depends on you. You. Just you." He pointed his index finger at my chest.

"What do you mean, I should learn English? Can't you understand me?" I said.

"Not very well. I've noticed you struggle to understand what customers are sayin'. They don't understand what you say, either. This is between and you and me: Cindy wouldn't have hired you if she'd had her way." I was surprised to hear this, and asked what made him think so. "I don't know, but that's what she said to me. Again, this is between you and me. You know, she has trouble understanding you too."

He walked toward the door to greet a customer. I stayed at my place. English was a delicate subject in my household in India. For my mother's family while she was growing up, English was a hangover from the British colonial past. My grandfather was very English in his mannerisms. English was his first language, and for a long time his only language. Growing up, I had spent most of my time with my mother's side of the family. It was a household in which people who didn't speak English were ridiculed. Anyone with less or no knowledge of English was thought to be less intelligent.

My father didn't speak English very well. When he tried, my mother's father and her brothers made fun of his pronunciation. Although my father had a master's degree and a good job, he lacked confidence. He would hesitate to talk to my class teacher during parent-teacher conferences. Generally, he was hesitant to talk to anyone who might talk with him in English. My father wanted to be able to speak English so badly that he abhorred everything associated with the language. While English was the bane of his existence, my mother was very adamant about sending her kids to schools where they could learn to speak English.

I was a little chubby as a kid. Not fat, but I had some extra weight on my body, enough for my scrawny classmates to pick on me. They called me *motu,* the equivalent of being called fatso. I took it in my stride while I was still a kid, but when I moved into my teens, I didn't take the abuse very well, especially when they called me fat in front of the girls in my class. I am not sure if the bullying at school was the sole reason for it, but it was around that age that I started spending a lot of time in the British Council Library in my hometown. I would read and listen to English audiocassettes. I wanted to speak English like an Englishman, just like my grandfather, who spoke with a posh British accent. The English language became my tool to fight back in class and in general. I started reading the English dictionary and would write down the meanings of big words. Then I'd go to school and use at least five big words to show off in my English essay.

My teacher would give me the look that said, "You didn't write this, did you?" But I knew the meaning of all the words I had used, and I was ready to answer her questions. I became the kid with good English, and a favorite of my English teacher. In my high school, you could fail any other subject and still advance to the next grade, but if you failed in English you'd have to repeat the year. My friends became jealous of me. They stopped calling me names.

Around the same time, I became obsessed with the British accent. I discovered the Beatles. When I was not listening to *The*

Goon Show in the library, I was enjoying Paul McCartney on an audiocassette. I rode my bicycle amid scooters, motorcycles, jeeps, and cars on the busy streets of Lucknow. When I found myself next to a loud truck, I would sing *Don't let me down!* at the top of my voice. I might have embarrassed myself, screaming out the lyrics with my eyes closed, but I didn't care. When I opened them, the truck was usually gone.

People would yell at me, "*Chup angrez ki aulad!*" It literally meant, "Shut up you son of an Englishman," but what it really meant was, "Shut up you son of a bitch."

My friends and some of my relatives, too, had started calling me by that name, *angrez*. They thought it was odd that I only listened to, and sang, English music. I got hold of a Hohner's Marine Band harmonica. I had been playing harmonica since I was eight, but that ten-hole blues harp fed into the English-crazed phase of my life. I carried it in my back pocket and tried to mimic the tune of the Beatles' *Let It Be.*

In Lucknow, which is where the first Indian revolt against the British took place, in 1857, there is a historical monument called the British Residency. The ruins are surrounded by several acres of lush green lawns. It was my little England. For a five-rupee ticket, I could spend the entire day there. I would walk in and around the main residence, imagining what it would be like if the British were still there. Every once in a while, I would encounter an English tourist. I would talk to him and felt elated when he'd refuse to believe that I hadn't grown up in England.

"Mate, I can't get over your English," he'd say. In India I had thrived by speaking English. But in the United States, my English declassed me. When Ron told me I needed to learn to speak English, speaking to me in what seemed like a demeaning tone, I wondered if he was trying to feel good about himself. At the time I felt mostly hurt and confused, but looking at it later, I could see that perhaps, as a working-class black man, he was trying to restore some of his own honor by stepping on me, a newly arrived, powerless immigrant—one marginalized community member oppressing the other.

CHAPTER TEN

Colleagues

The next day on the bus to work, I thought of Rupa, the middle-aged woman who worked in my parents' home. She washed dishes, swept and mopped floors, ground spices on a large piece of stone, and picked out the stones and bugs from the rice and lentils. She wore clothes passed down by my mother, and ate our leftovers from the day before. Her wages had started at five dollars a month and reached twenty dollars a month in the ten years that she worked for us. It wasn't that my parents didn't pay her well; that was simply the going rate. She lived with her husband in a small hut made of mud and bricks; it had a thatched roof with a tarp on it to keep the place from flooding when it rained. She bathed and washed clothes at a public tap.

I always wondered how she managed to run her home on the amount of money she made. She would often run out of money ten days into the month and ask for more to buy food or medicine. She would promise to pay it back at the end of the month; by the time she got the salary for the next month, she owed us half of it. The cycle would then continue—she would get a hundred rupees and return the fifty that she had borrowed over the course of the previous month.

Rupa's husband, Manoj, was an alcoholic who often beat her after getting drunk. He did a variety of odd jobs, but mostly he drove a cycle rickshaw. He spent the money he earned during the day drinking cheap liquor at night, and then fought with Rupa. Rupa often didn't show up for work.

She would complain that her husband was out of work, and that as a result he abused her and beat the kids. Sometimes she couldn't take it any more and would fall sick. We tried to help by giving Manoj part-time jobs, which would change things for a while, until Manoj started causing problems again. It made us angry when Rupa didn't show up for work for several days in a row. I remember my mother telling her that she had a month to get her act together, or she would fire her. I didn't know then that someone would say the same thing to me one day.

Back at the store, it was a slow Tuesday evening. Jackie had requested not to work the evening shift for a couple of weeks due to some personal problem, so Cindy told Ron and me that we would work together and close the store. Since Ron was training to be a store manager, he couldn't say no when Cindy asked him to work Jackie's shift. He was supposed to take the initiative and be ready for any crisis that might occur in the store.

The only people in the mall that evening were the store employees who stood at the entrance and waited for customers, and a group of six or seven kids walking around in hooded sweatshirts. They looked to be in their early teens. They jumped the stairs, slid down handrails, and yelled at each other. Then they walked into our store and dispersed in six different directions. It didn't seem like they were looking for anything in particular. I stood behind the counter and watched. Ron waited a few minutes for them to leave. They were flipping cell phones closed and open, taking pictures of each other with the phone cameras.

After a few minutes, Ron said, "You guys need help with anything?"

"Nah, we're just lookin'," someone answered, and they continued playing with the phones, pulling them out of the display shelf as far as the elastic string would let them.

When they began to become a nuisance, Ron walked up to them and straightened the phones. "You kids ain't got no homework or something?" Ron made it clear that the kids needed to leave.

"I finished my homework before I came here. I'm just chillin' now," one of them replied. But the group got the message and left the store.

"Looks like they are having fun in the mall," I said.

"They're just goofin' around," he said. "Y'know how kids are—restless and curious."

I nodded.

"Got any kids?" he asked.

"Not yet," I said. "Not ready yet."

"Yeah, do it only when you're ready, y'know—I'm tellin' you this with some experience." He said it with a serious face.

"Yeah, I know."

"Yep—I made the mistake and had kids too early, and then got divorced, now I'm stuck with paying child support," he said. "It ain't fun, that shit is no good."

"What's child support?" I asked, not quite understanding.

"All you need to know is that it's a good way of staying broke for the rest of your life."

I looked at him in need of more explanation. He said, "You pay a percentage of your income to support your kids if you get divorced."

"Really?" I said. "How long does that go for?"

"Long time, until they are eighteen," he said.

"Wow, that's a long time."

"Yep, it's for the people who get their girlfriends and wives pregnant and then realize they don't want the baby ... they walk out on their families because they don't want the responsibility of raising a kid, but they can't get away from the financial responsibility. The law requires them to support the kid until he or she is eighteen."

"I didn't know that," I said.

"Yeah, it's mostly young teenagers who goof up when they're in high school. I'm one of them. Now you know why I got high blood pressure?"

"I didn't know you had a blood pressure problem."

"Yeah!" He sighed. "I get tired pretty quick, and don't feel good after a long day at work." He leaned against the counter with his hands behind his back. "Docs say I shouldn't worry too much."

"You don't look old enough to have high blood pressure."

"Well, I am forty-seven."

I shook my head.

"Yeah, man, it's hard not to worry when you do two jobs to make ends meet." He continued. "We had bought a house a few years ago, and now we are struggling to pay the mortgage. My wife also works, but she got demoted from her manager's position. It's a big dent in our income."

When I asked him how long he had been married, he said, "Ah, this one ..." and looked at the ceiling with one eye closed, as if to think. "Seven some years. It seems like a long time though."

"What do you mean this one?"

"Oh, I've been married three times. I got kids from all of my wives, and grandkids too."

"Wow, you are forty-seven-years-old and you have grandkids."

"Yeah, I know. That's what they tell me. I started early," he said. I looked at him, and he continued, "I was a player when I was younger, always had too many girls, y'know. I didn't have to try very hard. They'd come to me on their own. I've dated all kinds, black, white, German, Colombian, Korean, but y'know what? All of them are after your money. If you aren't careful, you'll go bankrupt. Y'know what I am sayin'?" I nodded.

He continued. "Now I'm married, I needed to settle down. But I had fun when I was younger. It's awright to have fun when you're young, but when you marry someone you gotta make sure you don't marry a dumbass. Y'know what I'm sayin'? You don't want someone who already has three kids from her previous marriage. I mean if you got three of your kids, and she got some of hers, that's a lotta kids. You ain't gonna save a dime, y'know what I mean?"

"I know what you mean."

It seemed as if he needed someone to pay attention to him, and take an interest in what he had to say. Since he was opening up, I asked him more questions about his experiences, his life, and his interests. He answered them with great zeal, in stark contrast to the way he responded when I needed his help finding a product.

"What do you do when you go home, Ron?"

"I ain't got no energy after I get off work." He looked at his feet. "After eight hours of standing, all I wanna do is sit in my Laz-Z-Boy chair and watch TV."

"I know, I am getting used to it myself. Standing for so many hours is hard. I never had to do a job that required so much standing," I said.

"What sort of education you got?" This was the first time Ron had shown some curiosity about me.

"I have an MBA."

"You kiddin' me?" He looked at me in disbelief.

"No, I am not," I said.

"Whatcha doin' here then?" he said with an animated face. "Get the hell outta here. You can get a better job than this with an MBA."

"I did much better than this in India, but my degree is not from an American university, and I don't have any experience working in America."

"Gotcha. Well, you can work your way up. You see what I'm sayin'? You gotta start somewhere."

"Yes, that's what I am trying to do."

A young customer who hovered around the cell phone wall interrupted our conversation. I remembered Cindy's warning that I had a month to prove myself. Ron, who was leaning against the counter, said in a hushed voice, "Lemme go make some money—I need it." He pushed himself away from the counter, making his belly bounce up and down, to make a move. I acted like I hadn't heard him and reached the customer before he did.

It had been a very slow evening, and I doubted if the store would get more customers before it was time to close. I asked the person if I could help him. He said, "I'm not sure yet, I am just looking, thanks!" I stepped away to let him make up his mind. I came back and stood next to Ron—he stared at the entrance with no expression. I realized that while I wanted to make this sale, and keep my job, I was nowhere as desperate as

Ron. I didn't have any kids, didn't have to pay any child support, and didn't have a mortgage or any other kind of debt.

"I think you are a better salesperson," I said to Ron. "You should try to sell him a phone." He acknowledged the praise with a smile.

After talking to the young man for fifteen minutes, Ron brought him to the cash register. Looking at Ron's expression— a winning smile—it appeared as if he had convinced him to get a cell phone. Ron brought a few boxes of cell phones out from the backroom, and displayed them on the counter. The customer, who looked to be a teenager, picked one and Ron started processing the sale. Both Ron and the customer looked very pleased—Ron was getting a sale on a slow day and the young man was getting a cell phone. Just when Ron was about to swipe the credit card, I heard him say, "Shit," under his breath.

He stared at the screen for a few minutes, and then I saw his forehead sweat. He blew air out of his mouth, and said, "I am sorry, man, I should've asked you if you were eighteen." He looked at the customer with an apologetic face, and said, "I can't sell this to you."

"I will be eighteen next week," said the customer.

"Yes, but you gotta be eighteen today," Ron said, "I am sorry for wasting your time. I shoulda looked at your ID a little more carefully."

"Can I come next week and get the phone?" the customer asked.

"Yeah, you'll be fine next week." The young man left without much fuss.

Ron turned to me and shook his head. "I almost had it," he said. "Now I gotta clear this mess, take the phones back, and void the sale."

He spent the same amount of time hitting buttons on the keyboard as he had trying to convince the boy to buy the phone; a huge quantity of paper came out of the little receipt printer. Ron folded the papers up and stapled them together. "Cindy is not gonna like this," he said.

"Is it because you were not able to sell?" I asked.

"She doesn't like voiding tickets. She's fired some people in the past because they voided tickets for the wrong reasons, y'know," he said, and walked to the backroom with heavy steps, holding five cell phone boxes. When he came back, he said, "I don't know why they are putting me through these classes to be a manager. I got seventeen years of managerial experience, I know my shit."

"How long do you have to be in class for?"

"Six more months." He looked at me with a tired face.

"So you will be a manager when you finish your classes?"

"No, I gotta pass some exams, too."

"Is it hard?"

"It ain't hard, but they can make it hard for you."

"What do you mean they can make it hard for you?"

"Jackie seems to do better than me in exams. I don't understand how she gets better grades than I do. She don't know nothin', you see what I'm sayin'?" I looked on, blankly. "Yeah, maybe it's a woman thing, y'know?" he said. I looked at him, not comprehending what he was trying to say. "I know more than Cindy and Jackie, and they probably don't like that." Soon it was time to close the store. I hadn't sold much, but I felt I had gotten to know Ron. He seemed glad to have found someone who would listen to him.

Once a week, both Ron and Jackie drove to another city for their management training. Since their trainings were scheduled at the same time, Ron would give Jackie a ride. A few more months were left before they would both graduate, become managers, and have their own stores. That would mean better hours, every other weekend off, a considerable hike in income, less time standing on their feet because they would get a chair and a desk, and a team who would work under their leadership.

Ron seemed confident that he was better suited to be the manager of the store than Cindy. She was much younger than him, and had less work experience. He hated taking commands from her. His dissatisfaction about being an overqualified worker reporting to a less qualified and much younger woman often became apparent. He would speak under his breath when she told him to do certain things he didn't like.

Cindy was well aware of how he felt. I didn't think she treated him badly, or gave orders with a negative tone, but I could tell she got frustrated sometimes. She had been given the job of pulling this store out of the hole, and she was stuck with a foreigner who had no sales experience in America, and Ron, who thought he could do a better job than her as a manager. In India I had dealt with some disgruntled folks at work, who weren't good at taking commands or suggestions from employees who were senior in position but younger in age. Ron reminded me of them, but in America, understanding colleagues and the dynamics among them was more complicated than I had imagined it would be. Growing up, I had had some idea about the race issues in America, but it was only after coming to the United States that I learned how complex and subtle these issues could be.

About twenty days into the month that I had gotten the ultimatum from Cindy, I realized I still wasn't doing too well. My numbers were lagging, my knowledge of products was improving very slowly, and I was still having problems understanding customers.

Ron and Jackie helped me a lot, but they also got frustrated at my slow speed. Often, they would have to stop in the middle of a transaction with a customer to answer my questions.

While Cindy was trying to put our store in order, she was also taking classes to be promoted to district manager, a position in which she would have several stores and many managers under her. Once a week she would go for her training classes and arrive back at our store late in the evening. On those nights, she wore a black jacket and matching pants, and carried a tan leather laptop bag. On a normal night after training, she would look at the sales numbers for the day, and say something like, "Awright, guys, try to a get a couple of cell phones out this evening. We gotta sell, we gotta sell." Then she would spend an hour in the backroom, look at some paperwork, and leave.

One day when she returned from her training, she walked straight up to Ron, who was changing price tags.

"I need to talk to you. Got a minute?" she asked. He looked puzzled, but said yes and followed her outside. I watched through the glass windows of the store as she pulled out a pack of Marlboros, flicked open the top with her thumb, and offered it to Ron. He took one. She lit her cigarette and brought the flame of her lighter under Ron's chin. She didn't say anything and puffed a mouthful of smoke into the air a few times.

Ron took a long drag from his cigarette and kept the smoke inside for a quite a few seconds before he exhaled it through his nose. They both looked at each other—Ron wondering what it was that she couldn't tell him inside the store, and Cindy preparing herself to speak.

I noticed Ron saying something. Cindy looked at him and said something briefly, making eye contact with him and then looking away. Ron looked at her from the corner of his eyes, without turning to face her, as if he were expecting some bad news, but didn't want to hear it. He exhaled again, and spoke after a long pause. Then Ron was walking back, while Cindy stood there and smoked. She returned after a few minutes, and left soon without saying anything to anyone. I was going to be closing with Ron again. Jackie was supposed to leave in the next thirty minutes. Ron continued changing tags quietly.

After a few minutes, Jackie picked her purse up and logged herself out.

Just as she was leaving the store, she stepped back in and said, "Hey Ron, don't forget to pick me for the training tomorrow?"

Without looking up, Ron replied, "I ain't got no training to go to."

Jackie came back inside the store. "What didja say?"

"They took me off the classes." He continued putting on tags.

"Am I hearing you right?" she asked. He looked at her as if he were going to cry.

"Oh, man," she said and stood close to Ron. "When did you find out?"

"An hour ago. Cindy told me," he said.

"You know what, I don't think I am gonna make it either," she said. "I hope you have a better day." She slowly walked out.

Ron and I were left to close. He finished putting up tags, then stood near the counter, looking at the store entrance with aching eyes. I didn't know what to say to him. I also didn't know if it would be right, that evening, to ask him a question related to a product or request his help with something.

A couple of minutes later, a middle-aged African American man came in to pay his bill for satellite TV. I greeted him and took him to the register. It was a simple process—it required his ID, his money, and no help from Ron. While he stood there watching me feed information into the computer, he noticed Ron standing nearby, looking sad.

The customer said, "How is it going?"

Ron looked at him and said, "They don't think I can manage this store." The customer was done with his transaction and ready to leave. He hadn't expected his casual greeting to produce such a heavyweight answer. Surprised, he stopped, turned back and looked at Ron. Ron's sentence seemed to be loaded with pain, suffering, and disappointment. The customer stopped there for a moment, looked into his eyes, and said, "I hear you, I hear you, brother. I know watcha talkin' about."

It seemed like Ron had told him his life story in just one sentence.

The customer put his fist on Ron's arm pushing him gently, and said, "You take care of yourself, awright." His tone had a brotherly touch to it. I was moved. Ron spent the rest of the evening feeling sad and not selling anything.

I realized later that the conversation between the customer and Ron wasn't just a friendly chat between two men of similar age. It was a lot more than that. I was a newcomer in the United States back in 2004. Although I was curious about and fascinated by my adopted country and its people, I didn't understand the intricacies of racial dynamics. I knew about social hierarchy and discrimination from the way those things play out in India, but didn't know how they played out in the United States. Oftentimes, I didn't understand when a customer was rude to me. Not only did I not understand that people could confuse me with an Arab, but I also didn't know that being called an Arab in the United States was an insult. I paid close attention to what was happening around me, but every night I returned home with lots of unanswered questions.

The next morning when Cindy came to work she asked me, "So, how did it go with Ron last night?"

"He wasn't happy."

"They don't think he is doing too well on his tests, and asked me to take him off the training. I told him he could continue working as a sales associate, though," she said.

"What did he say?"

"He said that this is how it has always been with him. People don't wanna give him a chance, and blah, blah, blah—he threw away his cigarette mid-sentence and walked back to the store without waiting for me."

"It's sad," I said.

"I know," she said. "I like him, but he needs to do better than this if he wants to be considered for the manager's position."

Not knowing what to say, I gave her a blank look. She said, "Alright, since Ron won't be going to the training, I am going to change his work schedule a little bit." She walked back to her office.

When I got my timetable for the next week, I noticed I was going to work with Jackie for the next few days. I saw it as a positive change since she was a good salesperson and I might get to learn something. The next day when I came to work, I saw she was already there. We greeted each other, but she seemed sad.

I asked, "Are you okay, Jackie?"

"I don't know," she replied.

"What happened?"

"I am not sure how I will make it to the training since Ron won't be going to the classes any more. My car is still in the shop."

I had been working there for a month and I didn't know Jackie well enough to ask about the details of her life. She had only told me she was twenty-two years old and had no college education, but had six years of work experience—almost as much as I did. She was a single mother of a three-year-old kid; her son's father had walked away after getting her pregnant when she was nineteen. She had to set aside a good portion of the money she made at this job to pay the babysitter who took care of her kid while she worked.

She was seeing a man who would come and hang around in the mall and in front of the store while she worked. When he didn't come to the mall, he repeatedly called her at work. One day, when I got in an hour before Jackie was supposed to come, her boyfriend called several times to check if she had arrived. I got tired of telling him that she wasn't there yet. Finally, I told him I would make sure she called him as soon as she got to work.

Jackie arrived an hour later. She looked flustered. I told her that her man was looking for her. She didn't seem surprised, and shook her head. The phone rang again, only a minute after she walked in. I answered—it was him. She hadn't settled down yet—she still had her purse on her shoulder and her sunglasses on her head. I looked at her and pointed at the phone. She exhaled and snatched the receiver from my hand.

"Would you leave me alone, please?" she snapped, as she walked to the backroom.

A few shoppers walked into the store. She came back out, saying, "I gotta go, there're customers here." She put the phone back on the cradle and started helping people. For the next two hours there was a steady traffic of customers. When I got a minute to look at my watch, I realized it was almost time to eat. Jackie and I were both tired and ready to go on our lunch breaks, but we couldn't leave together. I asked Jackie if she wanted to go first. She said yes and clocked out.

After about fifteen minutes, I went to the backroom to get a camera for a customer. I saw Jackie sitting at Cindy's computer, browsing the Internet. Surprised to see her there, I said, "I thought you were going to eat."

"Deepak, yes I was going to eat, but I just realized that I ain't got no money to buy food today," she said. I wondered why she didn't have any money to get herself something cheap to eat. I asked if I could buy her lunch. She said, "That's really nice of you, I'll be sure to buy you lunch one day." I got her a cheeseburger and a large fountain drink.

Another time, when I came to work, I saw Jackie talking on the phone. I could tell by her expression that she was not happy. As I entered the store, I heard her say, "I gotta go." She put the phone down, but it rang as soon as it hit the base. She let it ring. She looked at me and shook her head as if to say, "He's at it again." The phone rang several times over the next two hours. She asked me to answer it and gestured to me to tell the person on the line that she was not there. Finally, when she got tired of the phone ringing, she took the receiver of the cordless phone and said, "I'll be back." She shut the door as she walked into the backroom.

For the next twenty minutes, while I stayed on the sales floor, I heard her scream, thump her feet, and bang her hands on what sounded like cardboard boxes. She looked very upset when she came out. I wanted to calm her down and ask what was wrong, but didn't know if it was appropriate. She was clearly distressed, and I worried that I'd make her more upset if I said something.

She didn't say anything to me either, just leaned against the counter, staring at nothing. We helped a few customers in the next half hour, and after a little while of not saying anything to each other, I asked, "Jackie, are you okay?"

"No, I am not okay," she said, and looked at me, angrily.

I knew her anger was not directed toward me. I didn't say anything and looked away. She came around and looked in my face and said, "Deepak, do I look like I go around kissing other women?" This took me by surprise.

"My boyfriend is accusing me of being a lesbian. He's drivin' me crazy, he always finds a reason to bother me—I can't take it anymore. I am tellin' you, I can't wait to find another man." As I looked on, she said, "He's been harassing me for the last month. He doesn't like it that I have a kid. I am trying to finish the training so I can become a manager, and become financially stable." Tears rolled down her face as she spoke.

I realized that while I was struggling to keep my job, my colleagues were dealing with much more serious problems. Working with Ron and Jackie made me think that in India I had only learned about the brighter side of America—its automatic cars, wide roads, tall buildings, drive-thru restaurants, and great shopping malls. I didn't know that behind the bright lights of this country there was a darker side, and that in that darkness there were people who struggled to make ends meet. There were people whose lives were not so rosy, and there were people whose problems were not unlike Rupa and Manoj's in India.

Rupa and Manoj were exploited because they belonged to a low caste. Because they belonged to a low caste, they worked menial jobs, and because they worked menial jobs, they couldn't provide good educations for their kids. As a result, their kids ended up doing menial jobs. It was almost impossible to break the cycle.

CHAPTER ELEVEN

Olive Skin

It was a slow day at work. Cindy suggested we change the price tags and dust the merchandise. Ron picked a section where all the TVs were. As he changed prices on the various items, he paused to watch the news. A newsperson was reporting about a terrorist attack in Iraq. After watching for a few minutes, Ron turned to me and said, "Why do you guys die in the name of Allah?" He laughed immediately after the question. I looked at him, and he said, "I'm just kiddin'." He seemed to have asked the question as if he were thinking out loud. He went back to changing tags. I didn't say anything to him, but I wondered why he had said "you guys."

An hour later, three olive-skinned ladies, covered head to toe in cream-colored veils—only their faces could be seen—shuffled in front of the store as if they wanted to come in, but seemed unsure. They waited for a few minutes and discussed something standing close to each other, allowing their bodies to touch. I couldn't see their faces, but it was clear that they were giggling behind the veils—it was apparent from their shoulder and hand movements. Cindy saw them and put on a curious face. I noticed they were gently pushing each other towards the entrance of the store.

After a few minutes of whispering in each other's ears, shoving, and giggling, they held hands and walked in. Ron stood out front, Cindy at the cash register, and I was helping another customer.

Ron tried to make eye contact, and asked in his deep husky voice, "Hayadoin?" With their eyes watching the floor they walked past him without saying a word. Ron studied the ladies, and shrugged his shoulders while he stayed in his place.

As they approached the counter, Cindy smiled at them. She asked, "May I help you find anything?" They giggled again.

"No, thank you, we're just looking." They stood around looking at the electronics with no interest, as if they were waiting for something, or someone. About ten minutes later, when I finished helping the customer, they approached me and giggled some more. When they came close, I could tell one of them was much older than the other two. She seemed to be their mother.

Cindy and Ron watched as they came close to me, and looked at each other as if they had no clue what was going on. I smiled and asked, "Can I help you?"

"Yes, but we are not looking for anything from this store," one of them said.

"Okay," I said feeling curious.

They glanced over their shoulders as if they wanted to make sure no one was listening. "Are you a Muslim?" one of them whispered.

"No, I am not," I said. I didn't understand what they were looking for. I realized I didn't have my tag on.

I put it on immediately and when they saw my name, one of them whispered to the other, "He's a Hindu." Hearing someone call me a Hindu made me feel good in a way I hadn't felt in a long time.

Living in India, I only once had to prove to anyone that I was Hindu. Otherwise, my religious identity never even came up. The scene brought to mind the one exception, an incident in India when I was denied entry into a Hindu temple because the priest refused to believe that I was a Hindu. Holly and I had celebrated our honeymoon in Puri—a small town in southern India famous for its beaches and Hindu temples. One day, Holly and I wanted to pay a visit to one of its temples and stood in a mile-long line of devotees to enter. After about two hours, our turn came. A hairy, bare-chested priest, with copious amount of yellow paste smeared across his forehead, was guarding the entrance. He was accepting the offerings—flowers, sweets, and donations—and then sprinkling holy water on the heads of the devotees as they entered the temple. Our turn came and we presented ourselves before him. He looked at me. Then he looked at Holly. His eyes shifted between my wife and me, rapidly.

"No, not you," he said in a sharp tone.

"Why not?"

"This temple is for Hindus only."

"How do you know I am not a Hindu? My name is Deepak Singh. Do you want to see my ID?"

"I know you are not a Hindu!" he shrieked. There were thousands of people waiting behind me. I felt humiliated and angry.

Growing up in a Hindu household, I woke up every morning to my mother praying in front of Hindu gods and goddesses. The tinkling sound of a little bell in her hand, the chanting of Hindu mantras, and the smell of incense came to my mind when I thought of my mother. I was born in a Hindu household, had a Hindu name, and enjoyed the privilege of being a Hindu in India— where Hindus are in the majority. I had friends who belonged to different faiths, but I never knew what it was like to not be a Hindu.

I was shocked to have my religion questioned for the first time. The priest was lucky that my mother was not with me. I am sure she would have slapped his face for saying that to me— the son of a devout Hindu mother who follows every ritual and fasts three times a week for three different gods.

"Of course I am," I said with irritation.

"You married this Christian woman," he pointed at my wife without looking at her.

"How does that change my religion?"

"Just go away, you are nobody. We didn't even let in Rajiv Gandhi," he said in a disparaging tone, referring to the former prime minister of India. "He married an Italian." Before I could say anything in my defense, he shoved me aside to let the next devotee in. Holly and I were both upset.

Several years later, at work in an electronics shop in America, I seemed to have caused a problem by not being a Muslim. The ladies in the store looked gloomy and said, "No, it's okay, we'll go somewhere else."

I insisted, "No, really, tell me what it is."

They looked at each other again, and then one of them said, "We were hoping you would know where to get halal meat." That put a smile on my face. Since they were so reluctant to talk to me, it made me think that they could not have approached anyone else in town who would know where to find meat butchered according to Islamic rituals. I was impressed that their guess had been almost right. In order to know what they wanted,

I had to be from somewhere in the Middle East, Pakistan, Bangladesh, or India, and be a devout Muslim. Since I grew up around Muslims in India, and knew a few Muslim people in Charlottesville, I happened to know of a place that carried halal meat.

"Yes, I know," I said. Smiles swam across their faces.

"You do? Where is it? We've been eating only vegetarian food since we didn't know where to get it." I asked them where they were from. "Pakistan," they said. "We are on a student exchange program at the University of Virginia." When I learned where they were from, I switched to Hindi. The ladies opened up and got comfortable with me, except that the mother kept pulling on the sleeves of the daughters, nudging them to leave. The girls didn't care—they were excited to be able to speak with me in their language. I was excited to talk with them too, since I had never met Pakistani women before. I was amazed to see how similar our interests, customs, and languages were, despite the fact that the politicians had made us look like worst enemies.

"Lucknow is famous for kebabs, did you know?" I said.

"I have heard so. That makes me want to eat kebabs right now."

"I know, same here. Do you guys watch Bollywood movies?"

"Yes! Amir Khan's our favorite. Love him!"

"By the way, I am a big fan of Wasim Akram. People love him in India," I said.

"Oh my god, we can't miss a single cricket match between India and Pakistan." During the half hour we spent reminiscing about our lives in India and Pakistan, I noticed that their mother pinching their arms, suggesting that they should hurry up. I also realized that Cindy was getting frustrated watching us talk for such a long time. It was funny that the girls' mother and my boss were not happy with us talking so freely, for entirely different reasons. Cindy must have thought I was wasting my time with them and not helping other customers. The mother wanted to leave because she thought it was inappropriate for her daughters to socialize with a strange man in a public place.

When it became too much, Cindy said in a sharp tone, "Hey, Deepak, could you change the price tags on the merchandise when you get done?" The ladies realized that they might have gotten me in trouble, and that they shouldn't have been talking for so long.

The mother looked at her daughters with a frown that said, "Look, I told you, you've been here way too long." They said goodbye to me in a hurry and started leaving. As they walked out, one of them turned around and asked if we carried digital cameras. Cindy's expression became less cross. Now the ladies had become customers. I talked to them for another twenty minutes and helped them find a product they would like. They ended up buying a camera, a memory card, and a pack of AA batteries. Cindy smiled as they walked out with a bag full of electronics. I felt good about myself that I managed to sell so much to people who hadn't come to shop.

After they left, Cindy came to me with a happy, but curious expression. "Hey, I wanted to ask you if those people were your relatives. You guys looked so happy to talk to each other."

"No, they weren't. They were actually from Pakistan."

"And, you're from India, right?" she asked, trying to remember.

"Yes, I am from India, but Urdu and Hindi have the same grammatical structure, so it was easy to speak to them."

"Do what, now?" She looked at me as if I'd spoken in Hindi, or Urdu.

"I mean the ladies spoke Urdu, which is the official language of Pakistan, and I spoke Hindi, the official language of India. There is a lot of similarity between the two."

She gave me a look that suggested she hadn't heard of either of the two languages before. After a long pause, as if she were trying to process the information, she said, "Cool! Could you say something in one of those languages? I'm curious ... just wanna hear you speak."

"What do you want me to say?"

"Hang on a second." She called out, "Ron, Jackie, come watch this." Both of them came and stood next to her.

"Go on Deepak, say, 'What's your name?' in Indian."

Everybody looked at me as if I were going to pull a pigeon out of a hat, or do a dance that no one had seen before. Cindy burst into a hysterical laugh when I said, *"Aapka naam kya hai?"* Ron and Cindy watched me dumbfounded.

When she recovered from her laughing fit, she said, "That was so cool, Deepak!" I didn't know how to react to such an overwhelming, rather odd response to a sentence that more than half a billion people speak in India on a daily basis.

The next day, Cindy came to me looking puzzled, holding what looked like someone's CV in her hand. "Hey, Deepak, do you know where this guy is from?" She pointed at the name, Reza Yousefi.

"Looks like this person is from somewhere in the Middle East, but I don't exactly know which country."

"That's what I thought, but I wanted to double check with you," she said.

After that, every time Cindy had a question that had anything to do with the Middle East, Muslims, or a language that wasn't English, she would come straight to me and quiz me as if I were her one-stop encyclopedia on the Arab world. I personally didn't have any objection to being labeled as a Middle Easterner. I had tried to clarify that I was from India, and had made an effort to point out on several occasions in an indirect way— since she'd never asked me my religion—that I was a Hindu, and I was from India. She never seemed to have understood exactly what that meant.

In my teenage years in India, I had lots of Muslim friends— Arif, Imran, Wahid, Naeem, Atif, and Alam were the closest, among many other acquaintances. They shared their food with me, took me in their homes, and invited me to have dinner in the days of Ramadan. They trusted me and shared their secrets as if I were one of their own. They would ask me if it would be appropriate to ask a Hindu girl out if they had a crush on one. We watched Hindi movies together, sang along with Bollywood music, and played cricket. We rewound John Lennon's "Imagine" on the cassette player several times to try to write down the lyrics, and enjoyed listening to the Rolling Stones' "Satisfaction," and Elvis's "Oh Baby." We sat very close to the TV to be able to see Steffi Graf's shapely legs when she played tennis, enjoyed watching Pete Sampras hitting aces, and expressed our amazement at Maradona's dribbling skill.

On lazy winter afternoons we lay on the roof on our backs and talked and dreamed about going to New York one day. We wanted to visit there together and see the Empire State building, walk through Times Square, and enjoy the bright lights. We wished to go to a place that was halfway around the globe, but somehow we never bothered to learn about or plan to visit Fallujah, Majra, or Baghdad, even though they were much closer to India. Cindy had assumed that, since I was from India, I must have relatives all around the Middle East, and that I must know everything about the culture and the language there.

This sort of thing was also the case with a lot of people I knew in India. An average Indian person's only source of information about the West was a cheap American movie. That's what they saw, and that's what they believed. All the soft-porn movies playing in dilapidated Indian theatres had white women in them and so people often thought every woman in America was loose.

I kept thinking of ways I could tell Cindy and my coworkers about Lucknow—my hometown—and India in general. They seemed to have a wrong impression of India, and a skewed sense of its geographical location. Cindy heard only about bomb explosions and suicide bombers in the Middle East, and that's what she thought of when she imagined those places. One day I pulled up an image of an Indian mountain resort on the computer. I wanted to show Cindy where I came from. I asked Cindy to take a look.

She said, "Wow, that's really built up."

"What do you mean it's built up?"

"I thought it was all desert."

I told her India does have desert, but also has mountains, beaches, more than twenty-two official languages, different religions, different seasons, and thousands of years of history. She exclaimed, "Oh, yeah! Look, I didn't know all this, Deepak!" She seemed curious, and asked, "Hey, listen, I wanted to ask you this: Are there a lot of monkeys in India?"

"Yes, there are monkeys in India."

"Coz, y'know, I was watching this show where they had to go to India. And, man, there were monkeys everywhere, like, on streets, on the pavement, on the walls. Do they run around like that all the time?"

She looked bewildered. "Isn't it true?" she asked.

"That's true! Actually, monkeys come into the cities because the trees are being cut down in the forests. They don't have a place to live."

"Aren't they, like, dangerous?" she said.

"They can be if people tease them, but in the Hindu religion monkeys are considered to be the reincarnation of Lord Hanuman—the monkey god. That's why most people feed them and just leave them alone, even if they cause some damage."

"Wow!" she said with her mouth wide open. She stared at the floor for a few minutes. "Let me go get some coffee, and I'll be right back." She walked out. In a few minutes, she returned with a smile.

"That's cool, Deepak! So, do you mind if I ask what religion you are?"

"No, I don't mind at all. I am a Hindu." She looked at me in need of more explanation.

When I didn't say anything else, she said with her forehead wrinkled, "Um, I'm sorry—who?"

I didn't know how to explain and had no idea where to begin. I tried to keep it simple. "It is a religion followed by 80 percent of the population in India. It's called Hinduism," I said.

Ron had been overhearing the conversation between Cindy and me while he walked around us. When he heard me say something about religion, he came over and said, "I spent a long time in I-raq when I was in the military. They're all Shiites there."

He looked at me and said, "Are you, too?"

I was in the middle of explaining to Cindy that I was a Hindu, and didn't expect him to interrupt like that.

Cindy looked at Ron irritably, and said, "No, no, no, Ron, let him explain, he's not that. He said he's a Hindu. It's different. Let him explain."

"Oh, I'm sorry for interrupting," Ron said.

I tried to explain my religion to Cindy. She seemed to be curious and wanted to learn more about me. After that she always asked me if people celebrated Christmas in India, if it snowed in India, about different festivals of India, about arranged marriages—she seemed to be fascinated by my foreignness, and I enjoyed telling her about my country.

When I think now, after several years, of my conversations with Cindy, it makes me realize that she was trying her best to understand me, my background, my culture, and my newly arrived immigrant self. She and I were different from each other in more than a thousand ways. Somehow we had ended up working with each other. When I look back now, I feel quite lucky to have had her as my boss. She taught me many things, things that were relevant not just on the sales floor, but also in life.

CHAPTER TWELVE

Camera King

"Deepak, you got paid. Here's your check," Cindy said in a matter-of-fact tone and gave me an envelope. To her, it was just another check, but this was my first salary check in America, my first check that wasn't in rupees, my first check that had a dollar sign before the amount. I thought of my family and friends in India. I knew my parents would be happy and proud of me. I didn't show my excitement to my colleagues, slipped the envelope in pocket, and continued checking items off the inventory list as I went through the shipment. But I couldn't take my mind off it. I got into the bathroom and tore open the envelope. I was having déjà vu.

When I looked at the check, I immediately converted the dollar amount into rupees. To my surprise, the amount was actually lower than what I had made in my last job in India. It hit me, once again, that I had quit my job in India and had come to the United States. Why? The question haunted me. Not only was the check was pathetic, but also I had less than a month to keep this job.

I still wasn't sure how I could learn to be a better salesman in the time remaining in my thirty days of probation. To avoid the embarrassment of not being able to answer customers' questions, I kept unboxing the products in the backroom, and dusting and straightening the shelves. It made me look busy. Ron and Jackie didn't mind. I got the feeling that they actually liked what I was doing. I was doing them a favor by saving them the monotony of putting items on shelves. They were happy greeting the customers, answering their questions, pitching new items, and making sales. I knew that the only way to make more money was to do what Ron and Jackie were doing. I desperately needed to spend time on the sales floor.

I decided I had to stop being afraid of people. I put on a happy face and greeted every customer who walked in. I tried to engage them in conversation, asking them how their day was going, and telling them who I was and where I came from before I helped them with what they came looking for. This didn't work all the time, but my new friendliness was effective with a lot of customers. It also helped that not every customer needed help. Half of them had done their research and knew exactly what they wanted. My job was to just ring them up. Because I had been so disappointed with my check, I tried to ring every customer who came in.

I was getting over my fear of talking with the customers, but after two weeks Cindy brought me a sheet of paper and said, "Deepak, your sales have improved, but your dollar per ticket is very low."

"What does that mean?"

"It means that you are ringing too many people. That's okay, but you should try to sell them high-dollar items, too. That can help boost up your sales and the dollar per ticket. Awright?"

Not everyone came in looking for a five-hundred dollar TV, a thousand dollar projector, or an expensive laptop. The majority of customers purchased items under twenty dollars. Ron, Jackie, and Cindy were good at selling cell phones, but that required knowledge and experience. To sell a customer a two-year service plan and a cell phone, one needed a lot of confidence, which I didn't have at this point. Selling a cell phone was just as complicated as dealing with a customer who came to return one. I saw my colleagues looking frustrated at the mere sight of someone walking through the door with a cell phone box. The store and the employee both took a massive hit on their performance if a cell phone came back. Sometimes we couldn't recover from the plunge in numbers, even after the end of the day. When someone came in looking for a cell phone plan, I happily ushered him or her in Jackie's direction. I knew I was losing money by doing this, but I was just not ready to handle that kind of transaction.

I wondered what high-dollar items I could sell. There were lots of items in the store: televisions, boom boxes, satellite radios, computers, DVD players, cameras. But I didn't know how to sell a TV to someone who had only come in to buy a ten dollar ethernet cable. How do you convince a customer to spend twenty times more money than he or she wanted? I had no idea, but I had no option but to try.

On a Monday morning, a little after ten, when I was in the store with Cindy in the backroom, a middle-aged woman walked in. She looked at me and said, "Is your last name Chopra?" and laughed. I smiled and said no. It made me happy that she knew the famous author Deepak Chopra.

"What part of India are you from?"

I was happily surprised that she could guess I was from India, and that she hadn't assumed I was from the Middle East.

"You know India?"

"Oh, yeah, I love India. A few years ago I was in Rishikesh for a month. I was learning yoga."

"I am so happy to hear this. I'm from Lucknow. Have you heard of it?"

"You know, I've actually passed through Lucknow on my way to Varanasi from New Delhi. If I remember correctly, my train stopped at the station for thirty minutes." She smiled.

I couldn't believe my ears. She knew India, she knew Rishikesh, and she had learn yoga. She said she had spent half an hour in Lucknow. I almost cried from gaiety. I told her she had to go to Lucknow next time. I described to her what Lucknow looked like, its history, weather, people, culture, and kebabs. I talked so passionately about my hometown, mostly because I missed it so much, that she and I both forgot what we were there for. And then, I realized I was supposed to be the salesman.

"I am sorry, I'm talking too much. What can I help you with today?"

"Oh, not at all. It's fascinating stuff. I want to go back to India."

"You should, yes."

"I am looking for a portable DVD player. You guys have one?" My eyes lit up. We had portable DVD players in stock and they were a high-dollar item. I brought a few different kinds for her and she chose the most expensive one. It was two hundred dollars. Trying to hide my excitement, I rang it up, but just before I hit the total button, I mustered up the courage to bring up the camera.

"Would you be interested in a digital camera today? This one has 3.2 megapixels," I said.

"You know what," she stopped for a moment and then said, "I have been meaning to buy one for a long time. Go ahead and ring it up." I looked at her in astonishment. I couldn't believe that just my mentioning the camera had been enough for her to say yes. I scanned the camera box and the total jumped to more than five hundred dollars. It was an amazing sight. She grabbed the plastic bag with her stuff in it and thanked me for helping her.

"And thanks for the great conversation," she said, just before she left the store. I thanked her and brought up the screen on the computer to look at my numbers. I couldn't take my eyes off it. $528 it said. She had been the first person in the store that day. My dollar per ticket was 528—at least for that moment. The money on the screen was not the money I had made, but it was more satisfying than the paltry sum on my salary check. It was a confirmation, a reassurance, a glimmer of hope.

I reflected on my conversation with the woman and realized that I had been able to sell her the camera not because I possessed great knowledge about the product, or because I had several years of experience in sales. I had been able to sell it because I talked with passion and no fear in my mind. I had forgotten that I was a salesman and conversed with her as I would have done with someone in a coffee shop, on a street, or at home.

I needed to do that again. I couldn't be Jackie, Cindy, or Ron. I couldn't know what they knew. I couldn't sound like them and couldn't look like them. But, I could be myself, be Indian, be a foreigner, be a man who'd just landed in the country, be Deepak. I decided I needed to connect with the customers on a personal level.

Later in the month, all the employees had to be at a store meeting at nine on a Saturday morning. Cindy had a few sheets of paper in one hand and large of cup of Starbucks coffee in the other.

"We need to order more cameras. They are flying off the shelf. Deepak, what are you doing? How are you able to sell so many cameras?" she said. Ron and Jackie looked at me. I was a little surprised that she had brought that up first thing in the meeting.

"I don't know. I just ask them if they would be interested in a camera. Most of the time they say no, but sometimes they want to buy it."

"Awesome, Deepak," said Cindy with a big grin. "That's great. Keep it up. You've become the king of digital cameras." Digital cameras had become my favorite things to sell. They were packed in boxes, stacked up on the counter, ready to go. Most of the information you needed was right on the box, and there was not much to learn. Point and shoot. And, they weren't cheap. They cost somewhere between two hundred and three hundred dollars.

After the meeting Ron came to me and said, "Whatchu do with the cameras? Whaddya tell the customers?" I knew he wanted to know how I sold, but I didn't know what to tell him. I told him the same thing that I had said to Cindy: I asked customers if they wanted to buy one. He didn't think it was that easy. There was something else to the story, he knew. He watched from the corner of his eyes when I talked to the customers.

When a customer walked in, I didn't say the standard salesman greeting: What can I help you with today? Most of the time, they had a ready answer for that question: Just looking. They wanted to be left alone. Instead I asked them a question about something they had on them—a book, a shirt with a message, a bracelet, their hairdo, or a tattoo. They didn't expect a salesman in an electronics store to be interested in what they were wearing. I surprised them, and more often than not, they were happy that I was showing interest in something that was personal to them. Once I had their attention, I was able to start some sort of conversation. The camera was the last thing I talked about. I always talked about the person. I felt manipulative in some way, but often I was genuinely interested in customers. It was an opportunity for me to socialize with Americans.

CHAPTER THIRTEEN

Don't Buy It

I slowly got over my fear of talking to the customers, but I was limited to digital cameras when it came to selling high-priced items. The store was stocked with hundreds of other pricey items, but a lot of them required knowledge to be able to persuade a customer to buy them. Sometimes, I tried to sway customers from buying what they had their hearts set on and tried to get them to buy something else because I didn't feel confident about selling what they wanted. It only worked when I had something to offer that was comparable to what they originally wanted.

One Saturday afternoon, the store was busy with people who wanted to buy cell phones. Cindy, Jackie, and Ron were all busy, with multiple cell phones laid out before them on the counter. They were at the cash register, explaining to families what plans would work best for them. I was trying to stick to customers who were interested in things other than cell phones, but everyone I approached seemed to want a cell phone. I wished selling a cell phone were as easy as selling a camera—pick up the box, scan the barcode, swipe the credit card, and you are done. It wasn't so easy, though. I had seen Cindy, the most experienced and confident among us, getting flustered when she sold a cell phone plan.

The computer often crashed while the customer was choosing a plan, and whoever was making the sale had to call the hotline. I was getting better at talking to Americans in person, but the idea of discussing a four-line cell phone family plan on the phone with someone who spoke in thick Virginia accent gave me the jitters. I'd had the hotline people ask me whether they could speak to someone who spoke English. Sometimes, they'd just hang up as soon as I opened my mouth. It was nerve-wracking to have an impatient customer waiting in front of me and have someone hang up on me—at the same time. Every call to the service provider took at least half an hour, fifteen minutes of which was just listening to a happy tune while you waited for a human. Cindy usually put the store phone on speaker and tried to keep the customers from walking away by telling them how awesome their lives would be after they got this phone. She never stopped smiling through the process, but I knew she couldn't wait to finish the sale. I was not as competent as her. Not even close. Not yet.

Later that day, an African American man who looked to be my father's age walked in. I was standing close to the entrance. He came straight up to me and said, "Could you help me with a cell phone?"

I knew I couldn't, but I said, "Of course. What do you need?"

"I'm looking for a cheap plan. I've never had one, but I want to get one now."

"Okay," I said, and looked to see whether any of my colleagues were free to help. They weren't. I didn't want to tell him that I couldn't help him myself, so I looked at the guy and asked him why he wanted to buy a cell phone.

"Oh, everyone has one these days. People expect you to have one."

"I shouldn't say this," I said in a hushed voice, "but you are better off without one. Use your home phone instead. Just because everyone has one doesn't mean you should get one, too. I know the company would love to have your business, but I think it's important to advise our customers wisely. Unless you really need a cell phone, I don't see a reason why you should be stuck with a bill for two years."

I didn't want Cindy or anyone else to hear this. My job was to convince a customer to buy something he wasn't sure of. It wasn't my job to convince a customer not to buy something he had come looking for. The old man looked at me, surprised. I smiled at him, not sure how he would react to my suggestion. He kept quiet, his eyes fixated on mine. Then he spoke.

"We need more people like you in the world. God bless you." He squeezed my shoulder and said, "Thank you, man. Thank you for being honest with me." I smiled at him again and he smiled back. He shook my hand and walked away.

I stood there and watched his back until he mingled in the crowd. I thought about my interaction with him. He may have liked my advice, but I hadn't advised him against buying a cell phone because I was concerned about his money. I'd done it because I didn't know how to help him. But the interesting outcome was that he had left the store happier than everyone else who did buy a cell phone. It seemed like he had the impression that I was being honest with him, but I felt weird about it.

A week later, when the store was not so busy and Ron and Jackie and I were standing around waiting for customers to come through the door, the old man walked in the door again.

Cindy greeted him. He said, "May I speak with Deepak?"

"Sure, he's right there," she said.

"Deepak!" he said.

"Good to see you again, sir?" I said, unsure why he'd come back.

"I want your advice on something."

"Sure, what is it?"

"I am looking for a weather radio. What do you suggest?" I brought out a weather radio.

"Do you think this is a good one?" he asked me.

"I think so," I answered.

"Go ahead and put it in the bag."

I asked him whether he had batteries at home.

"No, I don't. Would you give me a pack of whatever kind the radio needs?" After the sale, he shook my hand and thanked me.

I thought about my interaction with him for days. It was amazing how he had trusted me. I hadn't had to try to convince him of anything. I don't know whether he was convinced by the radio I had sold him, but he seemed to be 100 percent convinced by me—Deepak Singh, the salesman. Watching him put his trust in my words made me think of something else: I decided that every time I'd try to sell to a customer, I would try to imagine that the customer was me. What kind of advice, recommendation, or sales pitch I would give to myself if I were the salesman? I thought about it. I would not deter the customer from buying a product, but I would try very hard to sell each one something that fit his or her needs. It would have to be a fine balance between being a great salesman and a good human being.

CHAPTER FOURTEEN

Foreigner

"Awright, Deepak, I want you to be our second key holder after Jackie," Cindy announced during a morning staff meeting one Saturday. Everybody looked at her in amazement. The man who had been given a month's notice to prove himself a few weeks ago was now being given the custody of store keys. "I am doing this because I trust you," she said and smiled, looking at me.

She told everyone she was going to train me to open the store. She wanted to have someone else who could do it so that if she couldn't make it to the store in time, so customers wouldn't have to wait, she would not get fined five hundred dollars by the mall authorities for not opening the store at ten sharp, and her boss wouldn't scold her. I felt good about being thought worthy of such a responsibility, but I was also nervous since I would be accountable for thousands of dollars' worth of merchandise in the store.

One weekday morning after she had trained me to open on my own, I saw several people waiting outside the store. It was mostly on weekends that people would come early, not during the week. As soon as I opened the gates, I got busy with people looking for batteries, a microphone, or something else. To make the matter more complicated, the store phone didn't stop ringing.

I was trying to balance attending to people in the store and answering questions on the phone. After a longish transaction with one customer who couldn't make up her mind about which credit card she should use to pay for her purchase, I picked up the ever-ringing phone; it was Cindy on the other line.

"Are you okay, Deepak?" she said in a panicked voice. She sounded like there was an emergency, or someone had told her that I was sick or had met with an accident.

"Yes, I'm fine."

"I've been calling for the last twenty minutes … Why weren't you answering?" I told her that I was alone and busy with six customers who had come in at the same time.

"I got a call from the district office that the store hadn't been opened until 10:30 in the morning," she said. I took a quick look at my wristwatch to see if it matched the wall clock in the store.

"Cindy, I opened the store on time."

While I was still on the phone explaining that I had done everything right, a customer who was hovering around the cash register with a battery pack, ready to check out, spoke up, "It's your branch down the road that's still closed." Everything immediately made sense. I thanked him, silently with my lips.

I told Cindy, "You can tell the district office that it's not this store, but the one down the road. That must be why there were so many customers lining up at our store." I could almost see her smiling on the phone.

"Thank you," she said. "I knew it couldn't be you. Looks like Ned has been partying last night, and he's probably still in bed—and yes, the district office needs to call the right manager."

Although I wasn't the best salesperson in terms of volume, in my short time working with Cindy I had never taken a day off, or turned up late for work. Ron, Jackie, and even Cindy would call in sick every once in a while—my kid's throwing up, I have to go to the court, my head's hurtin', were some of the excuses they would come up with. Jackie was famous for coming late—ten minutes, twenty minutes, and sometimes an hour late.

Ron would just do a no-call no-show, often because he'd look at his work schedule incorrectly, and confuse a workday with a day off. Sometimes he forgot the store keys at home when he had to open. I often found him sitting on a comfortable mall chair outside the store, waiting for someone to open the gates. When I told him that he was supposed to open the store, he would say, "Shit, I forgot it was my turn." He would heave himself out of the chair to go home and retrieve the keys, muttering, "I forget shit sometimes."

I didn't think I was going out of my way for the company by coming to work regularly and on time. It was not something I expected to get credit for. I got the feeling that Cindy appreciated my punctuality. She could rely on me. While Ron, Jackie and Cindy had lots of other things going on in their lives, I didn't have any kids or relatives in Charlottesville except for my wife who was always busy writing a paper, attending a seminar, going to a lecture, or a meeting with a professor. Most days, she started at six in the morning and didn't finish until midnight. So my only obligation, apart from spending time with her, was to work.

It used to be different when I was in India and working. Then, I would have to try hard not to arrive late at work. With five people in the family and one bathroom to share, it used to be a struggle to make sure I got my turn to shower in time before the water supply got cut off for the day. It was quite a process before I got to work each day—wake up before anyone else did, get to the dairy before the line was too long and fetch milk, come back and perform my ablutions, iron my clothes before my brother took over the iron, grab a quick bite of *paratha*—a fried bread— and stop in to pay the phone bill on my way to work.

In Charlottesville, I didn't have to go through such rigmarole—no waiting around for the bathroom, no queuing up to see milk being drawn out of the cow's udder, and no running errands on my way to work. On my days off, which were usually weekdays since Cindy wanted her store to be fully staffed on weekends, I would not know what to do with myself. Since Holly had to go to school, I would often find myself taking the number 7 bus to the mall. I would spend time looking around other stores—the Gap, J. C. Penney, Belk, et cetera. I would also hang out with the Indians who owned the cell phone accessories kiosk. I didn't get the time to do all this on workdays, because I was only allowed thirty minutes for lunch.

Cindy also liked that I always came to work neatly dressed— in an ironed button-down shirt and pants, clean shaven, and hair trimmed. She told me how she hated workers who'd show up wearing creased shirts, with tousled hair, and reeking of alcohol at ten in the morning. I didn't have any friends to party with, so getting up early in the morning and arriving sober at work was not so difficult. I was glad that my dad had inculcated good habits in me, and Cindy was happy that I hadn't picked up bad habits in America. It seemed to work out for both of us.

Cindy also appreciated my ability to understand an Indian, Pakistani, or Bangladeshi customer's language, or make sense of their accent. If she didn't understand them, she would smile and call my name, as if she were going to pull out an instant translating gadget from her pocket that would break the code. I would come and chat with them and help them find what they were shopping for. Sometimes, I noticed her looking at us, smiling. Often times, when I was successful helping the South Asian customers, she would give me a thumbs up in appreciation.

I seemed to have taken up a role as some sort of advisor for international customers. Although I talked to people from many different countries, my sales numbers weren't improving because I was only able to sell to Indians, Pakistanis, or Bangladeshis, and they were few and far between. One thing that did improve, however, was my confidence level.

Cindy's collegial behavior and a few successes here and there helped boost my morale. I felt I could stay afloat in the company if I managed to reach a respectable sales volume. I noticed that Jackie would ring up only eight or nine customers in the whole day, but her sales total would be at least a thousand dollars. I had had a few successes with camera sales, but I was still relying on small-dollar items—batteries, wires, tiny bulbs, doorbells, alarm clocks—while Jackie would sell top-dollar products. Out of ten people she talked to, at least two would get a wireless phone plan—sometimes a family plan that would give her a thousand dollar ticket from a single customer. If they didn't buy a cell phone from her, she would try to push a flatscreen TV, a laptop, or digital camera. If I wanted to sell as much as Jackie did in a short span of time, I was going to have to do something out of the ordinary. It seemed like a big challenge.

One morning when I opened the store, Cindy came in five minutes after me. She said she had to catch up on some paperwork and that she was going to sit in the back. It was a typical slow Tuesday—not a soul was to be seen in the mall. I stood at the edge of the entrance, waiting for someone to walk in. A brown-skinned man who wore rimless spectacles passed by, looking a little lost. A few seconds later, he came back with a map.

"Do you know where this is?" he asked, pointing at the post office, two miles away from the mall. I told him where it was and also told him that there was another post office closer to the mall.

"Oh, no, I don't want to go to the post office, I wanted to go to the landline phone company, across from that post office," he said and we both laughed. He was from Argentina and had just arrived in Charlottesville to study business at the University of Virginia. Since I wasn't busy, I asked him how he was adjusting and liking the new place, and if he was missing home.

He spoke English well, but without an American twang; I had no problem understanding him. After we'd spent fifteen minutes talking, I suggested he should look into a cell phone plan, since that would give him free talk time at nights and on weekends, unlike a landline connection, and the monthly cost would be almost the same. He smiled and said he'd thought about it, but was discouraged by the security deposit he would have to pay because he was a foreigner and didn't have any credit history in the United States. He was right about the deposit. That was one reason I didn't have a cell phone myself.

I told him I could run a credit check and find out how much he would have to pay. He hesitated at first, and said that he should just get the landline connection.

"I have seen deposits as low as a hundred dollars sometimes," I said, "and they give it back to you at the end of the year." He was still not sure, but came with me into the store. I copied details from his Argentine passport into the computer, and clicked on the submit button to see what would come up. The webpage went blurry and the spinning wheel came on. This only happened to indicate two things: either the Internet connection was being slow, or the person in question had bad credit.

When it stopped spinning, I expected to see one of two messages—either "Webpage not found," or that the customer would need to put down a five hundred dollar deposit. After several seconds, to my surprise, the screen showed something else: a zero deposit. It meant he could walk out of the store with a working cell phone in his hand in a matter of a few minutes. The best part—he wouldn't have to pay anything, not a single cent, if he chose to get one of the free phones that came with the plan. Since he couldn't see the computer screen, I waited for a few more seconds to tell him the result. I wanted to double check all the details—to make sure it was really his name and not the last customer's—before I told him the result.

"So, my friend, how would you feel about getting a cell phone with a working phone number, and not paying anything today?"

Confused, he said, "What did you say?"

"You heard me right. You get a free cell phone today," I said. He still looked baffled. I explained to him that he would have to pick a monthly plan, and a phone that the company was giving for free, but he would not have to pay anything in the store. He would get a bill for the minutes he would use.

The Argentine looked happy. He said the landline company would take a week before the phone would start working, for almost the same amount. I also suggested that it would make sense to have the phone with him rather than at home, since he was going to spend so much time outside his apartment. Now the man who had come in to ask for an address a few minutes ago was standing in front of the cell phone wall, picking out a plan for himself.

After he made up his mind, I programmed his phone, and called his new number to see if it worked. The man was delighted to see the handset vibrating and ringing in his palm. I gave him a receipt that said, "Paid $0.00. Thank You, Come Again." He stood there looking at it with disbelief.

He made a call from his new phone to one of his friends before he left the store, letting him know what had transpired in the last half hour. He waved goodbye to me with the hand that carried the store bag hanging from his wrist as he walked out, with a winning smile, phone attached to his ear.

Cindy came out running as he left.

"Did you just sell a cell phone?" I told her the whole story, and she said, "You know, I was watching you talk to him." I smiled, and said I was surprised that the system had came up with no deposit. She said, "Oh, I didn't tell you that the cell phone company sometimes gives the benefit of the doubt to someone who has no credit history."

I said, "It worked for me and the customer was happy too."

"Well, good job, Deepak."

She came around the counter and punched in her ID to see the sales total for the day. A big smile swam across her face. I saw her raising her one palm in the air. She held it there for a few seconds looking at me, waiting for something. "Come on, give me a high five," she said. She hit my palm with hers making a loud pop when I raised my hand.

After an hour or so, I saw another man walking by the store, looking lost. I walked out to see if I was going to be lucky again. This person also came to me holding a piece of paper, as if he were going to ask something.

"I am looking for this man," he said, pointing his finger to something scribbled in a handwriting that looked strangely familiar.

I looked at it closely, and realized it was my own name, written by me. I couldn't believe that a man I'd never met had my name on a piece of paper in my handwriting. The mystery was solved when he told me that he was from Argentina and that his friend had recommended that he come to see me. I must have written down my name for the customer amid the excitement of selling a phone, and forgotten about it. I hadn't been in the store for more than an hour, and I already had another cell phone customer standing in front of me. I picked out a handset for him, suggested a plan, rang up the box, and wished him a good day. He was out the door in less than fifteen minutes. My sales total reached $750.

As the day progressed, four more people from Argentina, each holding a piece of paper that had my name on it, came to the store—one after the other. Ron, Jackie, and Cindy brought them to me because the foreigners wouldn't talk to anyone else. If they saw me busy with someone else, they patiently waited. When anyone else offered to help them, they smiled and pointed their finger at me. By the end of the day, I had more than two thousand dollars in sales.

I went home feeling happy. I was very tired, but even more excited. Just when I sat down at the kitchen table to tell everything to my wife, the house phone rang.

I answered—it was Cindy. "I just wanted to say that you did a great job with those foreigners today," she said. I thanked her and noticed the difference in the tone and warmth in her voice since the first time she had called me. A few months ago she wasn't sure about me—the guy from India—and it was clear that my foreign accent, education, and experience had caused her think of me as someone who wouldn't be a good fit on her sales team. I was glad to hear her say that I had done a good job selling to the Argentines, and I hoped that what had worried her most about me would turn out to be a unique selling point.

CHAPTER FIFTEEN

My Name Is Deepak

My grandfather gave me the name Deepak, which means source of light. But no one called me Deepak at home. I was known as Deepu. It was short for Deepak, but it was more than that. Deepu was supposed to be a little kid, no more than age ten, a kid who ran around the block playing with other little Deepus. Deepu was not supposed to be a grown-up man. Everyone knew me as Deepu where I lived. No one knew who Deepak was. I was Deepak only at school.

There, no one knew who Deepu was. I wanted to keep it that way. I didn't want my schoolteachers or classmates to know that my nickname was Deepu. There, I was embarrassed about being Deepu. If there was a boy in school who also happened to be my neighbor, I begged him not to call me Deepu at school.

The two names came with two different personalities. I didn't want my teachers or friends in school to know what I did as Deepu. I didn't want them to know how Deepu's mother pulled his ears and paraded him before other kids in his apartment complex if he was caught doing mischief. I didn't want them to know how Deepu sang in his bathroom. For my school friends and teachers, Deepu didn't exist. There was only Deepak. Deepak was someone who always wore a clean white shirt and ironed blue trousers and a monogramed necktie, and he looked the same every day.

At school, I was always conscious of what other kids thought about me. There were girls in my school, and that made me worry more about how I spoke, how I laughed, whether my teeth were clean, whether my hair was neatly parted, and whether I'd left a wet drop on my crotch after peeing.

I loved Deepak. I didn't like Deepu so much. Deepu was timid, shy, inept. Deepak was confident, brave, and ambitious. I whispered my name to myself to see what it sounded like. When I heard someone call me Deepak, it put a smile on my face. It felt like someone was giving me respect. When a school friend came to visit me at home, and he called me Deepak, I looked around to see whether my friends in my apartment complex had heard that. I wanted them to know that I was not just a Deepu, a Deepu they could take for granted.

When I moved to the States, people pronounced my name different ways. The name Deepak has two short syllables, and I learned quickly that Americans couldn't say a name that didn't have at least one long syllable. The correct way to say Deepak is *Thee-puck*, but most people in America called me *Dee-pack*. The American English *D* falls in between the two Hindi *D*s, but I got used to that. When I introduced myself to Cindy, she asked me to explain how to say my name. She called me *Dee-pack*, which was not perfect, but close.

Ron never asked me to explain how my name sounded. When he said my name I always heard the letter *T* instead of *D*. When he addressed me that way, Cindy and Jackie giggled a lot.

"Ron, you're funny," they'd say. I didn't understand what was funny, but I didn't try to find out. Then, one day, on the notice board, I saw there was a note that said, *"Tupac, can you work this Monday. I forgot I had a doctor's appointment—Ron."* I didn't know anyone named Tupac who worked with us, so I asked Jackie who the note was for.

"Deepak, that's for you. Ron calls you Tupac, you didn't know?" She laughed. I didn't know what the name meant. Later that day, I learned that Tupac was a famous rapper.

I didn't know how to feel about being called Tupac. Ron continued calling me Tupac. Sometimes, when he called me Tupac in front of the customers, they would laugh and say, "Hey, that's easy to remember."

Ron didn't just call me Tupac in private—he also introduced me that way to the UPS driver, the FedEx guy, the mail carrier, and everyone else who happened to come to the store.

"This is my man, Tupac," he'd say. I felt there was a sense of camaraderie, friendliness in his manner. The people he introduced me to seemed to like it, too. I didn't grow up in America, so I didn't really know what it might mean to be called Tupac.

It got to the point that new employees in the store and people who worked in the mall started calling me just Tupac. When I told them that my name was Deepak, not Tupac, they said, "Oh, okay."

It bothered me that people were calling me by a name that wasn't mine. They hadn't asked me whether they could call me that. They had just decided on their own without ever thinking about how it made me feel. I wasn't sure whether they were drawing me close or ridiculing me. Ever since I had arrived in the United States, I'd had to adjust to a variety of changes in my life—food, language, weather, customs, culture. I had very little opportunity to act like my familiar self, or to express my feelings. I often wondered about my identity, and who I was as a person. When people called me by a name that wasn't mine, I felt like screaming, "Could you guys at least call me Deepak?"

CHAPTER SIXTEEN

I'm Straight Today

Just as my colleagues at ElectronicsHut had some idea of India but had never come into contact with an Indian, I had heard of homosexual people in India but had never actually worked with one or even met a person who was openly gay. One evening, Ron's wife called to tell him that something important had come up at his home. It wasn't normal for his wife to call him at work. Ron didn't give us the details of the crisis—he just wanted to leave. Cindy let him go, but she wasn't comfortable with the idea of me closing by myself. The checklist for closing the store had too many things for just one person. Count the money in the till, gather and sort out the sales receipts into three different stacks—cash, credit cards, and checks—vacuum the floor, turn off the TVs, lock all the expensive merchandise in the cage, take the money to the bank ... it was a long list.

Cindy called another store to see whether she could borrow an employee for the night. A few minutes later, a round-faced, blond man walked in, swinging a key chain attached to his index finger. There was something awkward about his walking style, but I couldn't tell what. He smiled at me as he walked by—in the way a newly married woman does to her husband on the first day of her marriage—and checked me out top to bottom from the corner of his eye. Some of his fingernails were painted pink.

He walked back and knocked on the backroom door. Cindy came out and hugged him. "Howyadoin'?" she asked him.

"Hot," he said, and fanned his face with his hand with fingers stretched apart. He then smiled and moved his torso left and right without moving his feet. Cindy introduced us. I said hi and Kevin smiled again, blinking a few times.

He looked at Cindy and said, "By the way, I am straight today." He opened the two top buttons of his shirt and revealed a black T-shirt that said *Pussy* in bold letters.

"No way," she said, and laughed hysterically. I stood there watching the two of them laughing with wicked expressions, without a clue what was going on.

Cindy went home soon after, leaving Kevin and me alone. I didn't know what to think of the guy; he was different from the other American men I had met so far. He didn't talk for the first fifteen minutes and kept playing with his phone. After a while, a young man wearing tight jeans came in to inquire about a product.

When he walked out, Kevin said, "Ooh, look at his cute ass." He took me by surprise. I'd seen men admiring other men's biceps, broad chests, or shoulders because they were envious that they didn't have them, but I'd never encountered a man admiring another man's buttocks in such a manner. I was amazed and curious at the same time.

I tried hard not to say anything, but when we were alone again, I asked him, "Kevin, do you mind if I ask you something?"

"Go ahead," he said.

"I am curious to know why you thought the man's ass was cute."

He smiled. "It's because I thought it was cute," he said and started playing with his phone again. He hadn't answered my question; I stood there in need of more explanation.

"I mean, Kevin, why do you like a man's ass?"

"I just like it," he responded without looking up from his phone.

"Why do you prefer a man over a woman?" I asked again.

"Oh, a man's ass is much tighter—" he said in the way one talks about a favorite dish and in the middle of the description starts craving it. His eyes sparkled with excitement as he finished the sentence. "Oh yeah," he said after a brief pause, nodding his head up and down in conviction. I didn't say anything and just looked at him.

A few seconds later, he smiled, clenching his teeth gently, and said, "And sometimes, it smells real good."

Kevin's mannerisms, walking style, and body language reminded me of *hijras* in India. *Hijras* have male bodies, but dress and act like women. Some of them have very masculine body shapes—broad muscular shoulders, big biceps, facial hair. They move around the city in groups and knock on people's doors where there has been a marriage or birth recently. They dance and sing and bless the newly wedded couple or the child, and demand money. Of all my encounters with *hijras,* none have been pleasant. They are known for shouting obscenities.

I had seen *hijras* who did not hesitate to take their clothes off—I mean all their clothes—if their demands were not met. I had seen them grabbing men's genitals in public, feeling their buttocks, and planting a kiss on a young boy's freshly shaved face. The sound of loud drums beating, and the echo of forceful clapping and singing, signaled their presence in the vicinity.

Once, in Lucknow, I was waiting for a friend by the side of the road. A wiry traffic policeman across the street was swinging his stick at the rickshaws to suggest that they should not enter that road. Rickshaws were not allowed on it during certain hours of the day. Most rickshaw pullers obeyed, and let their clients off near where the policeman was standing. The cop seemed happy and waved his stick majestically after each poor man turned around and pedaled away. A few minutes later another rickshaw arrived, but this one did not stop, and ignored the stick. The policeman ran after him and hit the hood of the vehicle with his stick. The rickshaw stopped, and the man who was riding on it got off, gesturing with his hand at the rickshaw driver to stay out of the confrontation with the policeman.

The cop was offended because they hadn't listened to him and had instead kept going. I watched the rider—he was a foot taller than the man in uniform—talking and explaining something. The policeman didn't care that he was much smaller in stature. It seemed as if the rickshaw driver were caught between two people who wanted him to do opposite things. It clearly hadn't been his decision to break the law. He had been forced to keep going by the client and the policeman wanted him to stop. After a few minutes of squabbling, stick-waving, and finger-pointing, the scene took an ugly turn. The tall man pushed the policeman, throwing him on the road. The cop got up quickly, swinging his stick at the guy, but before he attacked, the tall, broad-shouldered, muscular man took his shirt off. I had been watching all this from the other side of the road, glancing away every minute or so to look for my friend.

The next thing I saw was the policeman running away, through the intersection, through the red light, amid the moving traffic, as if he didn't care if he got hit by a scooter, motorcycle, or a car. I looked back to see if the big man was still there. He was standing there, calmly buttoning up his shirt, straightening the collar, rolling the sleeves back down. He got back in the vehicle, and gestured for the rickshaw puller to move. After several minutes, the policeman came back to his post.

I was curious to know what had made the policeman run, so I crossed the street to talk to him. He was sweating profusely and panting as he looked around for his stick, which had fallen from his hands when he ran off. I asked him what had happened, and why he had run away like that. He looked at me, swallowed, and waited to catch his breath. He wet his lips with his tongue, and peered around as if he were trying to make sure the guy was gone.

"That man had boobs, real boobs. If I had known the motherfucker was a *hijra*, I wouldn't have messed with him. I stay away from those people."

Although Kevin wore men's clothes, men's shoes, and worked in the same capacity as me, his behavior, language, and style only brought *hijras* to my mind—I couldn't think of any other comparison. His graphic description of how a man's body appealed to him and his openness about his sexual orientation were disturbing to me. In India, I had gone to an all-boys' college, and had never, to my knowledge, encountered anyone who was attracted to the same sex. My two good friends were A.J. and Pinto. I shared everything with them—problems, happiness, money, food, and sometimes we lazed around in the same bed. We would often hold hands or have our arms around each other's shoulders when we walked. Such intimacy was not looked down upon by society, and no one ever thought of us as homosexuals.

I had heard of gay people, but didn't know any personally. There was a park in the very center of Lucknow that was "infamous" for homosexual activities. It was believed that men who were looking for other men had certain signs, gestures, and body language to communicate to those with similar interests. They would come around the park after sunset, and hang around looking for what they wanted. Sometimes, when my friends came to play cricket in the park, we would notice that the gathering of families picnicking—children playing with balloons, ladies chatting and nibbling on food, listening to the music on a cassette player—would slowly be replaced by single men, fidgeting and hovering in various corners of the park.

We would continue playing until it got too dark to see the cricket ball; when it took too long to find it around the park, we would start winding up. It seemed that the darkness caused us to stop playing, and set the scene for a different kind of a game. Every once in a while the local newspapers would run a head-line like "Cops Nab Men Engaged in Nefarious Activity in a City Park." I didn't know then that I would meet gay people in America who didn't need to go to a park and be clandestine about looking for partners. Throughout the evening, Kevin volunteered information about his past love affairs with men.

"I was married to someone much older than me, but I found out the person was cheating on me, so I divorced him."

"You were married to him and divorced him?" I asked, trying to take in the information.

"Yes, I was married to him for almost two years. We lived together, but you know, things don't always work out." I looked at him in amazement. "I am very picky," he continued, "when it comes to dating. I only date white men and you know what? I'm going on a date tonight. We are going to a club, I brought party clothes with me so I can go right after I get off work."

Soon, it was time to close the store. Kevin went to the bath-room and came out wearing a body-hugging round-necked pink shirt and equally tight black pants. He dialed a number on his phone and said, "I am ready, baby, are you coming to pick me up?" He ended the phone call with a kiss.

A plump, short-haired woman called Leslie, who had smoker's voice, used to come and meet Cindy at work almost every day. She dressed as many men dress—button-down shirt tucked into her pants, a big round watch on her wrist and a fat brown leather wallet sticking out of her back pocket. She was a friendly person and Ron and Jackie seemed to know her well. She would often tell Ron in her deep voice, "You need to stop taking smoking breaks, or I am gonna kick your ass," and then laugh raucously.

She would bring food, drinks, and do other favors for Cindy. They seemed to be good friends; they would giggle, tease, and be tactile with each other. I had gotten used to her being around. Sometimes she would come to the store and hang around in the mall while Cindy worked. I thought it was really nice of her to do that—a friend helping a friend.

One day Cindy invited all the store employees to her home for dinner. Ron said Cindy did this once a year. I thought I was lucky to get the chance since I had started working only recently. After driving for twenty minutes and twenty miles, I arrived at the place. It was a big house. I saw Leslie on the front porch, standing in front of a steel stove-like structure, moving her left hand to clear the smoke rising from it.

When I got close, I saw she was cooking round flat cakes of meat on the grill. Cindy came out of the house, greeted me, and took me inside. After a few minutes, through the large glass window, I saw Leslie getting into Cindy's white Honda Accord and driving away. Out of curiosity, I asked Cindy, "That's your car, right?"

She replied, "That's *our* car."

When Leslie returned, Cindy decided to give everyone a tour of her house. She started on the first floor and showed us the living room and pointed towards a large kitchen that was separated by a four-foot high wall from the living room. We moved to another section of the house, to a room which looked like a study area. It had two desks with computers on them. She said, "That's my desk, and this one is Leslie's." She moved to the second floor, and took us into a large bedroom, saying, "This is our bedroom." She turned towards another corner of the house and showed us the bathrooms. While everyone else was admiring the nice tiles and the bathtub, it occurred to me that she had missed something.

When we started going down, we had to go through the bedroom again. I stopped her and asked, "Did you forget to show us Leslie's bedroom?"

Cindy gave me a smile that didn't look natural, and said, "This is *our* bedroom." This time the stress on the word *our* had an angry tone to it. I didn't ask any further questions. When we arrived on the first floor, Cindy turned to me, while everyone stood around and watched, and said, "By the way, Deepak, Leslie and I are a couple." She rested her gaze on me for a few seconds after she said that. I didn't have much to say in response except a meek, "Okay."

After a little while, she asked everyone to start eating. Ron decided he needed to smoke before he ate. He stepped out on the wooden deck. I decided to go and stand with him. He offered me a cigarette. I told him I didn't smoke. Ron puffed smoke out of his mouth and then tried to chop it off with his hand to avoid sending it in my face. I was curious and disturbed by what I had just learned about Cindy. Also, I thought I had made her angry by asking about the bedroom in front of everyone. Although she'd answered my question, I was still curious. I didn't have the courage to inquire about her living situation.

Since I was closest to Ron, and he had shared some of his personal life, I felt he had become my confidante, my sounding board. I thought I would ask him, but before I could say anything, he looked at me and said, "I thought you knew already."

"Knew what?" I said.

He took another drag, exhaled the smoke, and said, "That they're lesbians." He had a look of disapproval.

I said, "No, I didn't have any idea that was the case ... I thought that she was married."

"She was married earlier, but I guess she figured out she's lesbian."

"Those are her kids, right?" I asked to make sure.

"Yes, they are," Ron said, looking at her kids. "It's hard for the kids, y'know." I listened, and waited for him to say more. "It's hard to explain to a ten-year-old why your momma sleeps with another woman," Ron said. "Y'know what I'm talkin' about?" He looked at me with his mouth twisted in another direction to blow the smoke. Again, I didn't say anything. It was too much for me to take in. I was shocked to hear all this. Ron rubbed out the cigarette butt with his boot and said, "Let's go eat."

I took a plate of food and watched Cindy and Leslie. They looked happy together. This was the first time I was seeing them in their home. They acted a little differently than the way I had seen them behave at work.

They both seemed to have a good understanding—a smooth relationship. When someone said to Cindy that he liked the wooden deck outside, she said with a glitter in her eyes, "Yeah, I know, that was Leslie's project." And when someone suggested the cookies were tasty, Leslie said, "I ain't got nothing' to do with that. Cindy baked them."

I thought of a film in India that had featured two women who were in love. I remembered how many cinema halls were burned down, windows were broken, and posters were burned in all the major cities in protest of the film's release. Some Indians thought it was immoral, and that it might suggest that women should give up their husbands if they were dissatisfied with them, and that homosexuality was against Indian tradition and culture. People also thought that it was an act of perversion and that it might set a bad example for the younger generation. As these thoughts flashed in my mind, I watched Leslie and Cindy giggling, joking, teasing, and dipping their French fries in the same bowl of ketchup.

The next morning, Cindy and I were working together. Ron and Jackie were supposed to arrive later in the day. At first, I didn't try to make any conversation with her, thinking of what had transpired at the party at her house last night.

"Sorry if I upset you last night," I said.

"You did not." She smiled and went back to her office.

I felt I was getting to know Cindy better—not just as my boss and colleague, but also as who she was in real life. Before I had gone to see her at her home, I'd only known her as a store manager, someone who knew all about electronics and who was good at managing people. As she opened up to me and asked questions about my life in India, I inquired more about her life. We seemed to have developed an understanding that it was okay for us to ask each other ignorant questions—and that we would not be offended. She was very much my boss when others were present, but she often treated me as her friend when no one was there.

Over time, she started explaining to me how people thought it was not right that she was dating Leslie. She would often tell me, "I don't understand what the problem is. She is just like my husband. You know, we do normal things that a husband and wife do, we have a family, we have a house, we care for each other—"

After spending a few months with Cindy, my perception of people with a preference for the same sex had changed. I had a few more opportunities to work with Kevin, and I didn't feel so alienated from him anymore. We had become friends.

CHAPTER SEVENTEEN

Holly and I

A few months after I arrived in Charlottesville, Holly and I moved from the house we shared with other graduate students. The new place was a university family housing unit, only for married couples. The rent was affordable. And, it was on campus—a couple of minutes' walk from the bus stop. Holly took the university blue bus to her class and I took the number 7 city bus to my work.

Living in our own place had made things better for Holly and me. Our relationship improved. The new place was a one-bedroom apartment with a living and dining room. We didn't have to share the kitchen or the bathroom with anyone else. Every single corner of the apartment belonged to us. It was just the two of us and we were free and able to spend more time with each other. We weren't used to living together. Living with a woman, a wife, an American wife in a foreign country took some getting used to. It took Holly some time to get used to living with a man, an Indian man, a husband. She got used to my singing Hindi songs in the bathroom, and I got used to the house smelling like chili. I introduced her to Kishore Kumar, a famous playback Indian singer. She opened a whole new world of American cuisine to me. Our home began to look like a perfect blend of the East and the West. We often listened to the Doors while eating chicken curry on our little square dining table, with its traditional Indian hand-embroidered tablecloth.

I have a very clear memory of how we celebrated our second wedding anniversary. It was our first in our own place. We had planned to eat in one of the many fancy restaurants in Charlottesville. We also had plans for a movie after that. But it had started snowing that day, and it continued snowing the entire day. It doesn't snow much in Virginia, but when it does everything shuts down. We were quite disappointed that the weather had ruined our plans. Not only did it snow that day, but we also lost power for a while. Luckily, we had a gas stove. We cooked a good meal, and worked together to make *chapatis,* as we did many nights after I returned from work. Then we lit a pumpkin spice-scented candle and sat at our small dining table. We ate and talked and looked at the snowfall through our window. It was beautiful and it was one of the most romantic dinners we had had so far. We still talk about how that day turned out. It reminded us of our wedding in India, and the many dinners we had had during power cuts in India.

We were happy together, but once in a while Holly said, "This is not fair, that I'm alone on the weekends." She didn't like it that I had to work nights and weekends. By the time I got home most nights, it was close to ten. She wanted to spend time with me. I wanted to do that too, but I also wanted Cindy to be happy with me. I didn't want to tell her that I couldn't work weekends or nights. Once in a while, when I did get the weekend off, Holly and I would go for long walks around the university, or drive to the many vineyards around Charlottesville.

I often wondered how Holly felt about her husband being a salesman. Unlike the spouses of some of the members of Holly's cohort, I wasn't an engineer, a city planner, or a financial analyst. Every so often I asked her what she thought about my work at ElectronicsHut and if she felt embarrassed to talk about my work with her friends, professors, her mentors in the department. Nearly every time her friends invited us to a party, I found an excuse to not go. When I did go, her friends asked me about how things were at work, which was exactly what I didn't want to talk about, and exactly what they wanted to know. I knew their intention was not to annoy or demean me. ElectronicsHut was such a big part of my life at that time and there was no way they couldn't talk about it. But I found it annoying and became irritable.

Holly didn't like it that I didn't want to go to see her friends. When I told her why, she said, "Look, this is not your fault that you don't have a job you deserve. This is the system's fault. I want you to feel good about yourself." Her belief in my abilities and her love for me was a huge support. It did change my mind a bit about spending time with her friends. But still, I wasn't too enamored of answering their dozens of questions about my workplace, even though Holly assured me that their questions likely came from curiosity driven by their training in anthropology.

I didn't have my driver's license for my first few months of work. I took the number 7 to work, but on the way back it was hard to get the bus. After nine at night, instead of running every thirty minutes, it ran only once an hour. Holly picked me up almost every night until the day I got my license. She often called me at work before she left, and laughed when I answered in my salesman tone, "Thanks for calling ElectronicsHut, this is

Deepak, how may I help you?" I felt a little embarrassed when I heard her on the phone, but happy at the same time that I wasn't going to have to answer a tricky question about setting up a computer ten minutes before I closed the store. On the way back in the car, she had to listen to my stories about the various customers I had dealt with throughout the day. I knew it wasn't as interesting to her as it was to me, but she listened anyway.

Although Holly's friends and colleagues in the anthropology department were worlds apart from my coworkers at ElectronicsHut, working with people from different backgrounds in retail did help me understand Holly a little bit better. They might not have studied the same books as Holly and her friends, but they celebrated the same festivals and probably watched some of the same movies and TV shows. Every once in a while when Holly came to pick me up, she spent a few minutes talking to Ron or Jackie or Cindy—depending on who was working with me that night. Although I spent eight hours with them every day on the sales floor, they had more things to talk or joke about with Holly. I watched them talk with a smile on my face, and thought, "Of course. You are all Americans."

Holly's friendly behavior towards my coworkers, her short conversations with them, helped bridge the cultural gap between them and me. It gave them more things to talk about with me. At the time, I didn't fully realize that her friendliness with them was also because she, too, came from a working-class background. Holly was easing my way into American culture in more ways than I could realize at the time.

CHAPTER EIGHTEEN

All Hands on Deck

One day when I came to work I saw a notice hanging above Cindy's computer: "Inventory Tomorrow—All Hands on Deck." I didn't understand what it meant. I knew all of the words in the sentence, but had no idea what they meant put together like that.

Cindy came to work half an hour later. She had just walked in and hadn't put her laptop bag down yet. I had been thinking about the notice in the backroom and couldn't resist asking her. "I saw something about inventory tomorrow, but what does 'All hands on deck' mean?"

She was in the middle of taking a swig from her coffee mug. As soon as I finished my question she spat out a mouthful of coffee, creating a fountain-like effect, as if she had a sprinkler attached to her mouth, spurting the liquid in a wide circle. I stepped back a few steps to keep the coffee spray from hitting my face. I had not expected such a strong response to my question. She tried to stop the squirt, but her hands were tied up holding the coffee mug and the laptop bag. She got rid of both items, wiped her mouth, and burst into loud laughter, bending backwards, banging her feet on the wooden floor. I had no idea that asking about something that she had written on the notice board would bring about such a scene.

I looked around to see if anyone was in the store watching the comedy. Luckily we were alone. I took my glasses off, wiped away the coffee drops, and put them back on. Cindy was still spinning like a top, balancing on one leg, using the other one to hit the floor, and laughing.

After a minute or so, she calmed down.

"God, you're funny, Deepak," she said.

I looked at her, puzzled. I thought I'd asked her a serious question. She said, "Awright, 'All hands on deck' is a term that is used in the Navy. It means that everyone is required to be present for a particular job." She smiled and looked at me.

I nodded, since it made sense. "And tomorrow is inventory day. We do this twice a year," she explained, "and it may take several hours, depending on how fast we do it."

I said, "Okay."

She smiled again, and said, "Deepak, I am sorry I laughed out loud, but I thought it was funny you didn't know what 'All hands on deck' was about."

"I'm sorry. I just wanted to be clear."

"No, no, no. It's perfectly all right. I love the way you ask about things you don't know." She smiled and raised her thumb in the air at me, and walked into her office. Later in the day, when everyone else arrived, she called for a quick meeting. She explained more about the inventory process. She said it was going to start after the store closed, and could go on until two in the morning, maybe later than that. She looked around and realized that people didn't seem very excited about working that late.

She said, "Guys, bring your comfortable clothes with you—shorts, T-shirts, whatever it is—and get comfortable. Also I've ordered a lot of pizza, so there'll be food, awright?"

"How about beer?" asked Ron.

"No beer, Ron, but there'll be Coke, Pepsi, Mountain Dew, and Dr. Pepper."

Ron, who was leaning with his belly on the counter, said, "I was just kiddin'. I've done hundreds of inventories."

"Awright, guys, this is it. Come prepared tomorrow." Cindy ended the meeting.

The next day, Cindy gave everyone a handgun-type gadget that had a small keyboard on top, and a scanner in front. It was supposed to scan the barcodes of every product—if for some reason it didn't recognize the merchandise, the barcode number had to be manually entered.

"Awright, guys, I wanna be clear on something tonight. I don't want any funky stuff, awright? Do not skip scanning something. I've assigned the scanners in each individual's name," she said. Everyone looked at each other, and turned towards Cindy. "I have also assigned different sections of the store under different person's names, so there's no confusion. The auditor will know who did what, and he'll come and fire you personally if you try to be smart. Everything that you see in this store—fuses, buzzers, antennas, radios, TVs, speakers, cell phones, clocks—needs to be scanned and accounted for."

People looked around, up at the ceiling, and down at the floor. "Yes, everything, even that light bulb we bought for the restroom," said Cindy, "and I wanted to let you guys know that Leslie has agreed to come and help us so we can get outta here quickly."

Ron and Jackie said in unison, "Yay!"

Five minutes before the store was supposed to close, Cindy changed into a sporty red T-shirt, flaming red baseball hat, and light-blue shorts, revealing her pale skinny legs, which seemed to have never seen the sun. She looked at her wristwatch, and said, "Someone lock the door from inside, please—it's time!" Jackie closed the door, walked over to the media wall, and tuned the satellite radio channel to hip-hop music, cranking up the volume very high. Cindy looked at her, raised both thumbs up in appreciation, and bobbled her head back and forth to keep time with the music.

I had never stayed after the store closed. As soon as the clock hit nine, I watched everything change around me very quickly. Ron came out of the restroom looking very different; he wore a hat, a sleeveless shirt, shorts, and sneakers. It was strange to see everybody act differently at work. I was the only one who hadn't brought any clothes to change into—I was a little uncomfortable wearing my home clothes in front of all my colleagues. The idea of wearing shorts and some rumpled T-shirt at my workplace, a place where I dressed as properly as I could, was a little strange to me.

Cindy called Leslie on her cell phone and said, "Where are you? Get your ass down here. *Now.*"

She held the phone close to the loud music coming out of one of the giant speakers for a few seconds. "Everybody chant, 'Leslie, Leslie, Leslie—'" she turned the phone towards us. She said, "Leslie is gonna love this message when she gets it."

Leslie walked in a couple of minutes later. She looked at everyone with a funny face and said, "I am gonna kick everybody's ass in this room for leaving me such a message. Deepak, I'll spare you, because I know it must not have been your idea." She looked at Ron, with a mischievous expression.

"I didn't do it," he said.

"Okay, okay, it was me who recorded the music on your answering machine. What are you gonna do about it?" said Cindy.

Leslie looked at her and said, "It was so loud. It almost made me deaf." Everyone laughed.

We all got to work after some fooling around. The *beep, beep, beep* of the scanners filled the room. With the loud music it was hard to tell whose machine was beeping. Cindy climbed an aluminum ladder to scan the items shelved high up. Leslie sat on a small stool and took care of the products around the baseboards.

Jackie, Ron, and I, standing close to each other, were shooting our guns at the merchandise at eye level. Pretty soon the job became tedious. Looking at the barcode of each and every product and pushing the trigger of the gun to scan it lost its novelty in the first hour, and we had only covered 10 percent of the store.

"Man, this shit is boring," said Ron.

"You ain't lying about that," Jackie agreed.

"I always tell the truth, y'know," he said. "I ain't like you."

"Whatchu mean, you ain't like me?" Jackie looked at him.

"I'm just messin' with you," Ron said and let out a tired laugh.

She stuck out her tongue at him playfully and said, "Don't mess with me at this hour of the night, you hear me, you black ass?"

"I know, it's time to go to bed. I'm losin' my mind," he said.

"Hey, where's the pizza at? I thought we were getting food—" Jackie said.

"I don't know, but I'm hungry too," Ron said. I was listening to their friendly banter. I had never heard them talk like that. They were mostly quite formal and polite with each other. The monotony of the work, and the fatigue from working too long was getting the better of them. We had already worked our full shift, and the inventory process was going to add another five or six hours to it. Some of us were going to have to open the store at ten the next morning—only a few hours after we got off from counting the products. It was going to be miserable.

Around eleven, someone knocked on the back door of the store. Cindy shouted, "Food's here!' The pizza delivery guy had a stack of six large Papa John's pizza boxes, and a plastic bag that held four two-liter bottles of soda. Leslie and Cindy carried the food inside. Everyone gathered around the pizza boxes—pepperoni, chicken, mushroom—and picked a slice of their choice. We realized Ron wasn't there. He was still on the sales floor, scanning items. Jackie said to me, "Deepak, tell that black ass to come and eat." I had a pizza slice in my hand, and I was about to put it in my mouth.

I stopped and yelled over the loud music, "Hey, you black ass, come eat," and bit into my chicken pizza slice. As I munched on the thick bread crust and the juicy chicken, I watched everyone's faces become serious—they almost stopped eating, like something had left a bad taste in their mouths. I swallowed the big piece of pizza in my mouth, took a long swig of soda, and said, "Ah, that feels good."

Everyone watched me in a strange manner. Ron came in, dragging his feet. I said, "Have some food, Ron." He stared at me as if I had asked him to do something I shouldn't have. "Why do you look so angry? It's not my fault that the pizza arrived so late." Everyone looked at each other, and resumed eating slowly without saying anything. I sensed something was not right. I was getting an odd vibe from everybody. We spent twenty minutes eating, but no one joked as much as they had at the beginning of the inventory.

Just when we were supposed to get back to scanning more items, Ron said, "Yo, Deepak," and gestured to me with his index finger to follow him as he walked out the back door. We came out in the empty parking lot. The only cars there belonged to Jackie, Ron, Leslie, and Cindy. It had gotten much cooler outside since I last came out, about twelve hours ago. Ron brought me under the orange light of the street lamp in the middle of the parking lot. I had no clue what he had on his mind. I had forgotten to put on my jacket before I walked out, and I was shivering.

All four cars parked nearby had their windows covered with frost. Ron took out a pack of Camel Lights from his pocket, and lit a cigarette. He took a drag and blew the smoke up in the air, bending his head all the way back. He looked down at the giant Walmart truck passing through on the road below the parking lot. He gestured at it with his two fingers that held the cigarette, as if he were waiting for the truck to pass.

When the noise of the vehicle faded, he looked at me, straight into my eyes, "Don't ever call a black man a nigger." I could see sadness and anger in his eyes. I wondered why he had to bring me out into the cold of the night at such an hour, in an empty parking lot, to tell me this. He said, "Do you know that it is a derogatory term, and that it could get you in trouble if you said that to a black person?"

"Yeah, I do, but when did I do that?"

"You don't know? You called me a black ass half an hour ago," he said, getting angry.

"Yes, but—" I said.

"It means the fuckin' same thing," he said, fuming.

I looked at him, and realized that I had inadvertently hurt him. I tried to explain. "If I remember correctly, you laughed and didn't seem to have any problem when Jackie said that to you."

"That's different," he said and took another long drag from his cigarette.

I looked at him, not understanding how another person calling him a black ass was okay, while it was rude when I did it. Since he didn't clarify, I asked, "How is that different?"

"It's alright for a black person to call another black man a nigger, but not you, because you ain't black. You gettin' my point?" he said as I looked on. "I just wanted you to know this because, it's alright with me since I'm your friend and a colleague, but if you did that to someone you didn't know you'd end up with a broken nose, if not shot." He looked at me as he explained. "I'm done, let's get inside, it's fuckin' cold out here." He started walking toward the store, and I followed him.

Ron had taught me a lesson. I felt bad that I had caused him to be upset. It made sense of why everybody had become awkward when I called him to eat pizza. I went back to the sales floor, picked up my gun and started scanning barcodes, standing close to Ron.

"I want to apologize for what I said to you."

"It's alright."

"And thank you for the explanation. I've learned something today and I would not do that again."

He didn't say anything, and we continued scanning, sitting on the floor, next to each other for a while. A few minutes later, he said, "Yeah, man, I'm used to this shit—" I looked at him. "My wife is a white woman, if you didn't know. We went to this bar the other day, mostly white people go there. People got drunk and they started calling her a nigger lover and shit like that."

He stepped a few steps back from the wall and rotated his neck as if he were trying to keep it from getting stiff. "Yeah man, there are a lot of racist people around here," he said. "It's something I have grown up with."

"It's not good."

"No, it's not."

"How does it affect you in general, other than the fact it's not pleasant to hear such racial slurs?" I asked.

"You can only know that when you are a black man yourself."

"I am not black, but I am also not white, and since I didn't grow up in this country, I don't notice things that are not obviously racist."

"You know that guy in the other store, down the road? And do you know that he sells more than Jackie, you, and I put together?"

"I didn't know that," I said. "What does that have to with the color of his skin?"

"Exactly—" he looked at me with a sarcastic expression.

"What do you mean?"

"He is a white dude, and people don't trust you as much if you aren't white in this country," he said. I continued scanning, waiting for him to say more. After working with him for a while, I'd learned that I didn't always have to ask him questions; he liked ranting.

"You see where I am now after more than fifteen years of experience and several certifications?" I nodded. "It ain't easy, you see what I'm sayin'?"

"Right."

Talking to him made me realize that nobody had ever spoken to me about how they were treated as a low-caste person in

India. No one had complained to me that they weren't allowed to sit on a chair that was supposed to be for someone of high caste. I had never come across anyone who said he or she had been called a Dalit-lover because they married an "untouchable." I realized I had never been associated with the working-class poor in India. I had never sat down on a floor next to a person who cleaned the streets of Lucknow and had a heart-to-heart conversation. No sales boy in a grocery store in my hometown had ever told me anything about his personal life. My maid in Lucknow had never discussed how she felt about eating my family's leftovers and cleaning our dirty utensils every day for two decades.

I also remembered my friend Brij, whom I met while playing cricket on a street near my home in Lucknow. We were both twenty-one then, and had finished our undergrad college degrees. Brij was extremely soft-spoken, and very good at mathematics. His ability to divide, multiply, and add a large number of figures in his head used to surprise many people. I took pride in hanging out with him. He was the first of all my friends to get a job. I had introduced him to my other friends, and he soon became a familiar face in my neighborhood. Everyone liked him for his generous, helpful, and friendly nature.

A few years later, a friend of his friend told people in our neighborhood that Brij belonged to a low-caste family. Some of the boys who had started hanging out with him raised their eyebrows. Everyone wondered why he had never mentioned that to any of us before. It was strange. Most of the time it was possible to tell what caste people belonged to by their names, but Brij had a last name that was used by many high-caste families. He never talked about his caste, anyone's caste, or castes in general. None of our friends would have been bothered if they'd found out that he belonged to a low-caste family, but he had never told us about it—he had kept it quiet.

Everyone started talking. I got curious. I asked him one day if the rumor was true. He took a deep breath and said, "Yes, it is." I looked at him, waiting for an explanation. He said, "I didn't want people to think that I wasn't capable of better things in life, and that I might not be suitable for a certain job because of my caste. I didn't want people to judge me. That's why I never brought it up." He looked at me with tears in his eyes, and said, "Now that you know that I am a low-caste man, do you still want to be friends with me?"

"Of course," I said, and gave him a hug.

While I was engrossed in these thoughts of my past, Ron said, "It's almost two in the morning and everyone is still working, and there's no sign of things coming to an end." I had spent about thirteen hours in the store, surrounded by the music, the wall full of electronics, the carpeted floor under my feet, and the ceiling studded with fluorescent bulbs. Just then, Cindy announced that we'd be done in an hour. We spent the last hour making sure there wasn't anything in the store that hadn't been counted. All the scanning devices had to be hooked to a dock so that their data could be downloaded to the computer. The monitor on the PC displayed the numbers and names of the merchandise on a continuing scroll.

A few minutes later, Cindy shouted, "YESSS! It is perfect!" We started winding up—vacuumed the floor, threw out the pizza boxes, and got our clothes together. As we walked out to the parking lot, Cindy thanked everyone for staying late and getting the job done.

People started getting into their cars. Before the inventory started, I had asked Ron to drop me at home. He had agreed to do so, but after my goof-up, I wasn't sure if he would still take me home. Since he hadn't said anything about changing his mind, I wasn't sure if I should ask someone else to drop me off. But to assume that he wouldn't take me would be another mistake. I was also worried that everyone would drive away, thinking that Ron was taking me home. I didn't want to be stuck in an empty parking lot by myself at three in the morning.

Ron flicked open his cigarette pack one more time. Cindy said, "Awright gentlemen, see you tomorrow." Leslie and Jackie also wished us good night. Now it was just Ron and me. He looked at me and asked, "Is your wife coming to pick you up?"

I didn't say anything, and looked away, thinking the worst. He started laughing out loud; the laughter turned into coughing. He laughed for a few minutes, coughing intermittently. He bent forward, with his hand on his chest, and spat a big lump of phlegm.

He looked up and said, "You must have been wondering if I was gonna drive you back." I looked at him. His voice was getting wheezy.

I asked, "Are you okay?"

"I'm fine," he said.

"If you can't drop me, I can call my wife to pick me up," I said.

"You gotta be stupid to wake her up at this hour," he said, and threw the cigarette away. He got into his car, flicked the headlights on, turned the engine on, and said, "Get in the car, you black ass."

We laughed.

CHAPTER NINETEEN

Long Two Years

It was a usual weekday morning—mall-walkers doing their thing, kiosk owners getting ready for the day, girls in skimpy dresses reaching out to apply lotion to customers' hands, six-teen-year-old, pimple-faced Ben walking around with a plate full of samples of sugar-coated pretzels, Justin at the coffeeshop filling the mall with the aroma of freshly brewed coffee, and some happy music coming out of the central speaker system.

I opened the store with Jackie. There were no customers, so I browsed the Internet for a while, changed price tags, and dusted demo products. About an hour later I decided to take a five-minute break. Ron and Cindy smoked cigarettes and they took frequent breaks. I didn't smoke, so coffee was my excuse to take breaks. I had acquired a taste for American coffee by having a cup every day. After several hours of listening to the same music, answering the same questions, looking at the same products, a five-minute coffee break often felt like being granted parole.

On my way to Starbucks, I saw the UPS guy tilting his head to hold his cell phone between his shoulder and ear, pushing a cart loaded with familiar-looking boxes, moving in the general direction of my store. I remembered it was Wednesday—the day new shipments arrived. Everyone hated shipment day. They preferred to come in late in the day so they could avoid dealing with the tedious job of cutting open the boxes, matching every item on the list to make sure we had gotten what we ordered, running around the store figuring what stuff went where. It had to be done correctly since everybody knew how Cindy hated finding the wrong stuff in the wrong place. The teeny-weeny items were the most cumbersome—one-eighth-inch audio jacks, quarter-inch male-to-female connectors, cell phone antennas. Everyone sighed in unison when we saw a box full of a hundred little plastic pouches of different-sized cables that needed to be sorted into various categories before they could be shelved. When cutting open a big cardboard box, we hoped there were just two or three items inside, like weather radios, digital cameras, or routers. They were easy to grab and just plunk on the shelves.

Waiting for my turn to get coffee, I was hoping the line would move slowly so I'd have a reason to be out of the store a little longer. But Justin was moving fast that morning, preparing lattes, mochas, and frappes faster than ever before. Justin and I had gotten to know each other. Sometimes he didn't charge me for my drinks. A fun-loving guy, he enjoyed flirting with a Nepalese woman who worked at a kiosk across from his store. She was twice his age. She became awkward and shy when he commented on her long and flowing hair. While Justin just had fun teasing the woman, she actually liked him. I could tell by the way she looked at him and then shied away as soon as he made eye contact.

My turn came and I asked him how he was doing. Holding the steel jug under the nozzle of a large coffee machine, he shouted so I could hear him over the noise, "Ah, you know, same shit, different day." He then turned the knob off and asked, "How's your day going?"

"I'm getting started. Just saw a big pile of boxes going towards my store."

"Gotcha. I feel your pain, man," he replied, sliding my coffee cup towards me on the counter. "Hang in there." He pointed his index finger at me as he turned to attend to the next customer. I walked back sipping my one-dollar-eighty-cent coffee, thinking about what Justin was going through, and that it was true for me too—same stuff, different day.

When I got back, there was a big pyramid of cardboard boxes sitting in the backroom. Jackie took the initiative and started opening the boxes. She asked me to stay on the floor to help customers. I thought it was very nice that she had volunteered to put up the shipment. She had been going through some problems and had been keeping to herself. She wasn't as vivacious and happy as usual. I checked to be sure she didn't want me to help.

She said, "I'll be fine." As I walked out of the backroom, I turned back and saw she was trying to lift a box and talk on the phone at the same time. I left her alone and came back on to the sales floor.

A few minutes later, a young white couple and an old man walked in. They seemed to be together, but drifted in three different directions once inside the store, as if they were looking for different things. They grouped up, talked in a disinterested way, and then went back to looking some more. The older man had cold blue eyes and a wrinkled face. His clothes were scruffy, and his hair unkempt. The younger man had flame-like tattoos crawling up his neck from under his plaid shirt; he appeared to

be a painter because he was wearing overalls covered with splat-
terings of different colored paints. His boots also had paint on
them. The girl revealed her cigarette-stained teeth every time
she said something or smiled. I could see a yellow lighter tucked
under the strap of her red tank top, and a cigarette behind her
left ear. She paced between the two men every two minutes,
while they stayed in two different sections of the store. She
called the former daddy and the latter honey.

I asked the younger man if I could help him. "Nah, I'm just
looking," he said. He spaced the words quite far apart as if he
could be convinced to buy, depending on what I had to offer, and
whether it suited his needs and wallet. I took a few steps back to
respect his answer and space, but didn't leave him standing
there alone. After a couple of seconds I said, "We've got some
good deals on wireless phones at the moment. A free cell phone."

He looked at me immediately. "Free, you said?"

"Yes, free. It comes with a two-year plan."

"Which one of them is free?" he asked. I pointed out a couple
of phones.

"Hmm. Can you tell me about the plans?" he said. I grabbed a
brochure and showed him the cheapest monthly plan. It was just
under forty dollars a month. He took the brochure from my
hand to look at it closely. The girl noticed him showing interest
in a cell phone plan. She came close and stood next to him, cran-
ing her neck to read the brochure. I could sense a family-plan
sale—a two-phone sale, or maybe three. I mentioned that he
could add another line to his account for just another ten dollars
a month. The girl's eyes twinkled.

She said, "Yes, come on. Do it." She looked at him longingly.
The guy folded the brochure and gave it back to me. The man
seemed to be put off by something. I didn't know what.

"If you get two lines, you get two free phones," I said, thinking this might be alluring for the two of them.

"It's not the phone I'm worried about, it's the two-year contract. I don't wanna sign up for two years, especially when I'm not sure if we're gonna be together for that long," he said, wrinkling his forehead.

The girl looked sad, the man unsure, and I didn't know what to say. Usually, when people didn't want to buy a cell phone they told me that they didn't get any reception at their home, or that they were already locked into a plan with a different service provider. I had learned from Cindy how to handle such rejections. Most of the time I was able to come up with some sort of solution to whatever was keeping a customer from buying a cell phone plan. But when the guy said he wasn't sure how long he was going to be with his girlfriend, I didn't know what to say. I felt bad for the girl. I thought she must be feeling humiliated.

I was reminded of a similar incident that had happened when I was riding my scooter home to Lucknow after visiting a friend who lived ten miles out of the city. It was June and the wind in my face made me feel like I was engulfed by fire. I stopped to take my helmet off. By the side of the road, under a large tree, I saw a shirtless man yelling at a woman. The woman was sobbing. I looked at them and didn't think much of it. Then I saw the man give the woman a wallop to her head. I got off my scooter and went close to them. I asked him why he was mistreating her. He told me he was a farmer who worked on other people's farms and he hadn't been paid for the last three months. The woman was giving him a hard time for not bringing any money home, he said. I didn't know what the real story was, but I told him not to hit her. She continued crying, but didn't say anything in her defense. I stayed there for a few minutes, looking helplessly at the couple. Then, as the man sat scribbling on the ground with a twig, he told the woman that she could go with me.

"He has more money than me," he said. She looked at me. In her eyes I saw sadness, helplessness, anger, the feeling of being unwanted. I had stepped off my scooter to intervene and stop the man from tormenting the woman, but I found myself in the middle of a deep crisis. I felt horrible about the woman, the man, and about myself. What misery, I thought. Feeling helpless, I got on my scooter and drove off.

I spent the rest of the day thinking about the couple. It was easy for me to drive off and leave the scene, but forgetting about them wasn't going to solve their problem. Disturbed by the incident, I narrated the story to my parents. They listened. My father didn't say anything for several minutes, his normal response when he was pondering about something, usually a sad situation. My mother responds quickly. She said, "Poverty is the biggest curse."

Now at work in Charlottesville, I found myself in a similar situation. The man hadn't thought twice before revealing to me personal details about his relationship.

"But we've been together for almost two years," the girl said after a minute. "Haven't we?"

He looked at her, but didn't say anything. I stepped back to let them talk in private. In the meantime, the older man walked over. He saw his daughter standing close to the young man looking at his face while he looked in another direction.

She grabbed his chin, turned his face towards her, and said, "Well, if we break up before the contract is over, I promise I'll keep paying you my part of the bill."

He took her hand off his chin and put it down with his right hand. "What if you don't?"

"Come on, we've been together for two years. You don't trust me?" she said, holding his head with her hands to keep him from looking away. He grabbed her hands again, and moved them down, sliding them over his chest, his stomach. A silence followed. The girl kept looking at him, begging for a phone with her eyes like a child who promises her parents that she will behave if they buy her an expensive toy. The young man gave her a look that said, "I've heard that before, tell me something new."

The older man looked at me and shrugged his shoulders. I shrugged mine back. Then he spoke to the pair.

"Yeah, you guys have been going around for almost two years now."

The younger man turned to him and said in a sharp tone, "Dude, it's been a long two years." He stretched the word—*long*—long enough to stress that he'd had a rough time with her. He stared at the girl's father in a way that suggested he should stay out of this drama.

"I ain't gettin' in the middle of that," said the old man.

"Exactly," the young man said.

A real-life family drama was taking place right before me, under the fluorescent lights, amid the music coming out of the display televisions, satellite radios, and CD players. I wanted to get away, but the three of them kept looking at me as if I were some sort of witness, a judge or a counselor who was supposed to come up with a solution. I couldn't leave them.

I didn't know what to say to the girl every time she looked at me with pain on her face, after telling her boyfriend she had been with him for two years. I didn't have any words when the man explained how long those two years were for him, and I felt powerless when the frail father, looking at me with his sad eyes, said he didn't want to be part of the problem. I hadn't realized that pitching a product to someone could lead to such a nerve-wracking scene. There were a lot of things that didn't make sense to me. The older man felt bad for his daughter, but I wasn't sure whether he didn't have the money to buy her a phone himself or just didn't want to help her. Also, the girl wasn't shy about begging for a phone from her supposed boyfriend in public.

The guy seemed to have made up his mind not to get a phone for his girlfriend, but the girl didn't give up pleading. After about thirty minutes of begging, arguing, and explaining, the young man raised his voice and said, "Fuck it, I ain't gettin' no phone today." He stormed out of the store, leaving the girl and her father behind. The dad looked at me and shrugged his shoulders one more time.

I stood at the counter and watched them walk out slowly. I didn't know how to feel. I was more disturbed by their situation than I was sad to lose the sale. It bothered me to see the girl begging and not worrying about people watching. What troubled me even more was the helpless dad, who stood there and watched his daughter being ridiculed in public and couldn't do anything about it.

After they left it was time for me to take my lunch break. I wanted to talk about what I'd seen. I went to find my Indian friend Mahesh in the mall, to tell him. On my lunch breaks, I had been going to him and had gotten to know him quite well. He shared a lot of his personal life with me. He had been in the United States for five years. He had arrived on a work visa, as a software engineer, but had been laid off due to the bad economy.

After having no luck with jobs, he resorted to starting his own cell phone accessories business.

With his wife, he worked long hours in the mall. They worked together at the kiosk most of the time, but sometimes he left her alone to run errands in the city. His wife had recently arrived in the country and was recovering from the shock of learning that her husband was no longer a software engineer, which is how he had been represented when his family approached her family to arrange the marriage in India. Mahesh had confessed his guilt that his family hadn't told the truth to his wife's parents. It was his fault, he told me, since he hadn't revealed to his own family that he'd been laid off and was working odd jobs to survive. He also mentioned that he had apologized to his wife, and promised her that he would do his best to keep her happy. She seemed to have understood and was willing to cooperate with her husband in the tough times.

On my recent visits to their kiosk, Nishi had been complaining about working in the mall. She said it was like working on a street—people walking by watching you hawk your wares, stopping to take a look, being rude, accusing her of selling cheap stuff. This bothered Mahesh, but there was nothing much he could do. He told me how much he hated to leave her alone when he had to take care of things. He left the mall for a few hours every other day to get the car fixed, buy groceries, or gather stuff for their kiosk. She didn't enjoy being on her own. She'd had some bad experiences while Mahesh was gone.

Once, a group of young teenagers mobbed her kiosk from all sides, stole stuff, mimicked her Indian accent. When she tried to stop them they told her to go back to her country. She gave up, sat there, cried, and let them loot.

That day when I approached their place, I saw Mahesh standing very close to his wife. She had her head bent down on the counter of their three-by-three-foot kiosk, which was open on all sides. The multicolored faceplates from various cell phones hanging around it provided some privacy. When I got close, Mahesh looked up. His eyes were moist. He had his hand on his wife's head, which she continued to keep down. By the movement of her ribs, I could tell she was sobbing. He didn't say anything, just kept looking at me.

After a few seconds, he took me aside and said, "I just booked our flights to India." I looked at him, surprised, since he hadn't mentioned anything about going to India recently.

I asked, "What's going on?"

"You know how she has a hard time dealing with people when I am not here. People ask stupid questions, say mean things, and she doesn't take it very well."

"Yes, I know. This has been going on for a while, right?" I said.

"Yes, but today when I'd gone to get some food for us, someone was really rude to her. It made her very upset." I looked on, curiously. "This man who'd bought a car charger for his DVD player from us two months ago came back to return it. Nishi told him she couldn't give him his money back because it's been more than a month—past the thirty-day return policy date."

"Okay, what happened then?" I said.

"The man created an ugly scene and started using F-words at her," Mahesh said and he lowered his glasses to wipe the tears. "You know I've never raised my voice to her and that man humiliated her in public. I wasn't even here." He looked away, choking up.

I took a deep breath and put my hand on his shoulder. He looked at his wife, and said, "When she told me all this I immediately called the travel agent and booked two one-way tickets to India. I just can't take it anymore. She doesn't deserve all this." I realized Mahesh was very upset and emotional. I told him I would come back later to talk to him. I walked back to my store without telling him what I had witnessed an hour before.

I thought about what a contrasting set of events I had witnessed that day—one man had humiliated his girlfriend in a store full of people, while the other man thought it was humiliating that his wife had been insulted in public. I took the last swig of my coffee before I threw the cup away, and prepared myself for the next four hours of work.

CHAPTER TWENTY

The Golden Quarter

I was starting to feel like I was getting the hang of things at work. Cindy wasn't as frustrated with me as she used to be, and I had gotten to know my colleagues better. Also, I seemed to have developed a mental map of the store in my head; I realized I was able to locate a particular product placed anywhere in the store almost immediately. This was something I hadn't tried to learn—it had just come to me over time, the result of being there for eight hours a day, five days a week.

I was impressed with myself for having developed such a good sense of what was where at work, since I still couldn't find things at home. I would often lose my belt, my sock, or my underwear, and end up emptying the entire wardrobe in an attempt to find it. But I also didn't make half as much of an effort to put things where they were supposed to go as I did at work. I figured the danger of my wife divorcing me was much lower than that of Cindy firing me. My efficiency at work was a good manifestation of an old proverb in India. Literally translated from Hindi to English, it would mean something like: fear makes love happen.

My sales figures were slowly making it to a respectable level. I had learned a lot by watching others—Cindy's skill at convincing the customer by giving a live demonstration; Jackie's cheerful, loving, and friendly chatter; and Ron's ability to make customers believe how much knowledge and experience he had. I was learning something from everyone. It seemed to be the best—the only—way to learn.

For the past week or so Cindy had been talking about the golden quarter a lot. "You gotta be ready for the golden quarter." "You know what happens when we approach the golden quarter." "Things get really busy in the golden quarter."

One morning when she was returning from her daily visit to the coffee shop in the mall, she turned to me, put on a cheeky smile, and said, "Deepak, I'm surprised you haven't asked me what the golden quarter is all about yet."

Acknowledging that she was teasing me, I smiled and said, "Well, I was going to, but I thought I should wait until you put that coffee cup away." She laughed loudly.

She said, "Very good, Deepak, very good." Later in the day she called for a meeting. Everyone gathered around the counter.

"I hope you guys are aware that the holiday season is around the corner—a time when most Americans go into debt buying gifts for their friends and family," she said. "I don't have to tell you how most businesses look forward to this time—the golden quarter. They plan ahead, since this is the opportunity when *you* don't have to try too hard to sell; people readily spend everything they have." She put on a big grin. "I want to make sure my staff understands the seriousness of this big occasion because you know what it means for you."

As we looked on, she said, rubbing her index finger on her thumb vigorously, "Yes, money, money, money, that's what's it's all about. Everyone makes huge commissions." She said there were going to be a lot of changes in how things worked at the store. A new line of products would be introduced to cater to demand in the market. The sales floor would have to make room to accommodate shipments.

She said the head office had given her permission to hire three more people for the golden quarter. Cindy mentioned that the three new people would be seasonal employees. They would only be hired for the holiday season—October to December— but if they performed well, they could be considered for longer-term employment. She said we would have to help train them. She conducted the interviews and after going through a few people she hired a twenty-year-old African American man, Cameron; a nineteen-year-old white girl, Paula; and a forty-year-old white man, Tom.

Cameron's last boss had given him a negative reference, but Cindy liked him and said she wanted to give him a chance. Paula was very short—well below five feet—and had a round face and blond hair. She had done a variety of sales jobs before, but had been a waitress most recently. She acted as if she knew the job and the place as well as if she had been working with us for a long time. Tom was not Cindy's choice. She had received orders from the district office to hire him. Apparently he had been working for our company as a manager, but was demoted and sent to our store. All three started within a few days.

I wondered if the sales would go high enough to keep six people busy on the sales floor. Oftentimes it was hard keeping two of us occupied; time and again we found ourselves rearranging the items, changing the price tags, or standing around chatting when there was nothing else to do. Worried about all of the employees making enough sales to earn decent commissions,

I asked Cindy, "Do you think it will be busy enough to keep all of us occupied?" She laughed, and said, "You watch, Deepak. On Black Friday, I find it hard to even go take a pee—it's that busy."

"Black Friday—what's that?" I asked.

"You don't know what Black Friday is, Deepak?" Jackie asked, looking at me with raised eyebrows.

Cindy laughed again, and said, "He's from India, don't you know?"

I stood there, shifting my gaze between Cindy and Jackie, trying to figure out what I had been missing, and what the joke was.

"Oh, Deepak," Cindy said, trying to recover from her laughing spasm. "Awright, Black Friday is the day after Thanksgiving. It is the biggest day of the year for retail businesses. There are huge discounts on lots of things, and it is the start of the holiday season in America. Most people start their Christmas shopping on Black Friday, and keep going til Christmas."

She took a swig from the coffee cup sitting next to her. "And all the stores open at five ... and some even earlier."

"You mean five o'clock in the morning?"

"Yes, Deepak, that early," she said. "And everyone needs to be at work at four because people line up outside the door much before we open." I couldn't imagine people coming to shop at five in the morning. The way Cindy was talking she seemed to be preparing to deal with not just a handful of customers, but a mob.

"In order to be ready for that day, I have a list of things to tell you," she said. Everyone looked at her. She smiled, with a sparkle in her eyes. "I've got a strategy, and everybody let me know if you agree with this, or you wanna do it differently, awright?" she said. "Since it's going to be crazy busy, no one's gonna get a chance to talk to any of the customers. You'll just be clerking, ringing people up—that's all." It was very rare that customers came in to buy something and one of us didn't have to answer a question, or help them find exactly what they needed. It was unimaginable that people would just grab stuff off the shelf and bring it to the cash register. I was having a hard time believing everything Cindy was saying about Black Friday.

"So, my suggestion is that we divide up the sales that day among the six sales associates. There are three cash registers, and everyone can take turns ringing people up, because I am tellin' you, you gonna get tired of standing in one place constantly for hours." This surprised me. I thought everything was based on performance in America—you work hard, you move up—and not about sharing your wealth with someone who didn't try as hard as you did.

Most Americans get up in arms about socialism—distributing your income among others—but it appeared that Cindy had something else in mind. I had been trying to do well, and wanted to be competitive. I looked at Ron and Jackie to see what they thought of this idea. Apparently, this was their first time working on a Black Friday too, but they seemed to understand Cindy's ideas more than I did. They didn't protest. The newly hired employees didn't mind either, but I was a little apprehensive.

I asked, "So, Cindy, will it be fair to divide the sales even when some people tried harder than others?"

"That's why I am leaving this to you guys to decide. I've seen this before and I know what it's like. It's better to team up and help the store make more money, and in the process everyone else makes money too," she explained. Although I wasn't too excited about sharing my sales with everyone else, especially on a day when I could sell a lot, I agreed with Cindy. No one else said yes or no—it was assumed that Cindy's plan was approved.

"Now, since it's going to be a very busy day, and you will need a lot of stamina running back and forth fetching products from the backroom, standing long hours on your feet, I am cooking a lot of food for you guys," said Cindy. "Expect to see a table full of goodies when you arrive in the morning." I didn't know how to react to everything. It felt exciting, challenging, adventurous, and unbelievable. And it didn't seem as if Cindy was done with the meeting, since she was still sitting on the countertop, going through her notes.

"And, yes, I wanted to tell you about the people. You'll have to be very patient, very patient. You will encounter some real nasty customers that day." Ron and Jackie looked at me and nodded, as if they knew exactly what she meant, while I looked at her inquisitively. I didn't understand what she meant by people being nasty at five in the morning.

"Yes, a lot of people who come to shop that day are generally in a bad mood. They are hung over from excessive drinking the night before, they've eaten too much, and some of them can be really rude—" she left the sentence half-finished to be amplified by our imaginations. She told us that we would need to work for at least twelve hours that day—4 A.M. to 4 P.M.—and some of us would have to stay until nine o'clock.

The store was closed on the day of Thanksgiving. Most of my colleagues were celebrating with their families who lived in Charlottesville, or drove to nearby towns to visit their relatives. Holly wanted to see her family, who lived in rural Pennsylvania, but this time she had to stay home, since I needed to work the next day—we could not have gotten back in time for me to work at four in the morning. Since she still wanted to celebrate, she decided to prepare the traditional Thanksgiving meal—turkey, mashed potatoes, gravy, cranberry sauce—for the two of us; we ate and talked about Black Friday. I asked her if she had ever gone to shop at five in the morning.

"No, I haven't, but it looks like I am going to do it tomorrow." She looked at me and smiled. We went to bed early that night. She was going to drop me off and then take a walk around the mall and check out the sales.

The alarm went off, and I got out of bed. I walked to the window and looked at the apartment parking lot below—it appeared unusually empty. I wondered if the people had already left to line up outside the stores. I took a shower quickly and got ready for the day. Soon we were on the road. I saw that all the stores had their blue, green, and red neon *Open* signs glowing, lots of people were gathering, and cars were shuffling in and out of the parking lots. Men, women, and children were walking on the sidewalks in herds as if they were performing some holy pilgrimage.

It reminded me of the epic festival of Kumbh Mela in India, when millions of Hindus travel for miles to take one holy dip in the sacred Ganges before sunrise to rid them of their sins. They fast for several days before the festival, and then perform long worshipping rituals after immersing their bodies in the sacred water. It made me think that the Americans were doing the same thing except they had been eating a lot the day before, and were now walking in the dark to immerse their souls in the material world.

We arrived at the mall, and my wife had to circle three times before she could find a spot to park. I had never seen the parking lot so full. There was a hint of deep blue in the sky, stars were twinkling, and it was still dark. The parking area was filled with the muffled sound of car engines running. People were sitting inside their cars, with the heat turned on, trying to stay warm on a chilly November morning; they had an hour to wait before the mall would open. As I walked across the lot, I saw through the fogged-up windows of the cars that some people were dozing—plopped on their seats, which were reclined to an 180 degree angle, their feet up by the windshields.

When I walked through the back door of my store, I saw a long table full of muffins, scones, cookies, cakes, chips, bagels, doughnuts, different kinds of sodas, a brown square cardboard box labeled *Coffee*, and plastic utensils. Cindy, who was sitting on her chair, had her hair freshly washed, but her eyes were still puffy. It seemed like she had spent the entire night preparing for this day. The lights on the sales floor weren't turned on yet, and the mall was dark too—only the backroom was lit.

In the next few minutes, the sales staff arrived. Before Cindy said anything about the food or eating, Ron filled his cup with coffee, and said, "I need to wake up." Cindy, who seemed to have forgotten to ask people to help themselves to food, said, "Oh, yeah, go ahead and grab a bite, y'all—it's gonna be a long day."

Everyone stood around with their hands wrapped around coffee cups, staring at the floor, not saying anything, as if they were in a zombie state. After a few minutes, when people had woken up a little more, Cindy said, "Alright guys, no one's ringing sales in their names—you ring it in my name, and I will split the total in six parts when the day is over." She gave us her password.

"I think there's enough food to last for the rest of the day and feel free to have seconds, thirds, fourths, as much as you want. Once the mall is opened, you're not gonna get a chance to relax," she said.

"The parking lot is full of people waiting to get in," Jackie said.

"Yep, I told you," said Cindy. "Go ahead and turn the lights on, it'll be time to open soon." Jackie flicked the switch and we moved onto the sales floor. It felt strange being inside the store with no one else in the mall but hundreds of people waiting outside to get in. It felt like some kind of a battle: Cindy, our commander, was prepared with her soldiers to defend against the enemy waiting to get inside the mall and loot our wealth. I felt a little uneasy about what might happen when the doors opened. I had gotten used to dealing with the customers in ones and twos, and felt nervous about a mob. We had to be nice to them while they were allowed to be rough.

As I was thinking of all this, I heard Cindy say, "Go ahead and open the doors." There was still no one in the mall. I opened the doors and stepped out to see what it felt like to be in the mall at five in the morning. All the stores were open, festive-sounding music poured from the mall sound system, and in the next minute, I saw a hundred or so people rushing in my direction through the hallway on my left. They moved fast, almost running, holding leaflets, brochures, and what looked like newspaper cuttings.

The last time I had seen a mob like this was when I went to the train station in Lucknow to see off one of my friends. It was in the early hours, maybe four or five o'clock—the sun hadn't risen. We had arrived early and hung around on platform number 1, drinking tea out of Styrofoam cups, waiting for my friend's train to New Delhi. We walked around, detouring around people who lay on the floor with their heads resting on bags or other sorts of luggage. About ten minutes later, when the train arrived, we saw about a thousand people pouring in from all directions. Their aim was to get on the train and occupy a seat before someone else claimed it.

In a country of more than a billion it is not surprising to see so many people at any given moment—it happens all the time. It was hard to believe my eyes when I saw hundreds of people heading in my direction at five in the morning in Charlottesville. They wanted to get into the store first and grab the items on sale before the store ran out. I quickly got back inside the store, and announced, "They're here."

In the next few seconds, the store was filled with more people than it could possibly hold. Young men, older men, young women, women who were not so young, teenagers, children, toddlers, and babies occupied every inch of the sales floor. I stood behind the counter, and watched them scan the store with their eyes, as if they were on some kind of mission, a treasure hunt. They were not just browsing, but hungrily searching, rummaging through each shelf, looking up, down, behind, and underneath every single section of the store. I tried saying hello to some of them, but they didn't bother even to look at me. Their eyes were set on something else. They wanted to be done with this store and move on to the next one.

In the process of moving, shoving, looking, and grabbing, they knocked down piles of toys stacked up in several places around the store. Within ten minutes they changed the way the store looked—price tags were torn off, displays knocked down, products that had been hanging on hooks lay on the floor, and the merchandise on the shelves was disorderly. Three of us, including me, were on the cash registers; the other three were lost in the crowd somewhere.

One lady, who seemed to have rolled out of her bed only a minute ago—she had lint stuck in her black curly hair—started bringing stuff to the counter. She had two little boys who were helping her grab things from different parts of the store. When I started to check her out, she said, "Hold on a second, can't you see I am still shopping?" I apologized, and waited. She kept bringing stuff until half of the counter was covered with her things.

"Awright, I am ready now," she said.

I began to check her out. I scanned for ten minutes, and I was only half done with her pile.

While I concentrated on keeping separate the items I had scanned from the items I hadn't, I heard a loud scream. "Listen bitch, you better keep your child's fuckin' hands off my boy's toys." I was startled to hear someone swear like that, and turned around to see who it was. Another lady with an enormous pile of toys was getting ready to check out next to me. Jackie was helping her bring stuff to the counter while she tried to keep her kid from running around. The other woman had a mean look on her face. Suddenly, the lady with me was standing face to face with her.

"You don't call me no bitch, you whore," she screamed back. "It's too early in the mornin', and y'know what? It's my fuckin' child and I ain't stoppin' him from gettin' anything he lays his hands on today. Am I clear enough, you whore?"

All hell broke loose. The next minute, the two ladies grabbed a Rubicon toy jeep, and engaged in a real tug of war, calling names, swearing, grunting, spitting, and screaming. I saw Cindy stepping aside and getting on the phone to call mall security. I didn't think that the guards would respond fast enough on a day like this, since there must be fights in other stores too. In the meantime, the two women carried on.

Finally, the lady I was helping gave up, and said, "Fuck this shit. I ain't spendin' another minute in this store. Can't deal with this woman no more." She stormed out, dragging her kids, while one of them yelled, "Momma, my Rubicon." The package was torn and the toy broken. I was left with a mountain of merchandise.

I looked at Cindy, who said, "Go ahead and void that ticket out," and exhaled in exasperation. The quarrel between the two ladies didn't dampen the shopping spirits of other people in the store. They continued prowling. I voided the ticket, and moved the merchandise that was strewn across the counter. After the fight, I noticed that people were more careful about not mixing their things with others'. They circled their arms around their stuff until someone checked them out and put it in a bag. I had never seen sales receipts the length of my body before. The machine wouldn't stop spitting paper.

People were on edge, irritable, and not friendly at all. The hour of the day had something to do with it, but it seemed there were other things that were affecting their mood. I recognized some people in the crowd who were regular customers, and who were usually patient and cordial. Even they seemed to be in the same mood as everyone else. It felt like the limited supply of the extra-cheap products, and a small window of time to shop, put everyone under pressure.

"You got that ten dollar digital photo frame in stock?"

"Yes, we do, sir."

"How many you got?"

"We have fourteen of them."

"I'll take all of them." It felt as if they wanted to buy all of them not because they needed fourteen photo frames, but because they didn't want thirteen other people to be able to get them.

"Hey, you got that ten dollar digital photo frame in stock? I need four of 'em."

"No, ma'am, we just ran out of them."

"Chrissakes, it's only six in the morning, and you are already out of them?"

"Someone just bought all of them."

"Really?"

"Yes, ma'am."

"God, someone's really desperate." They would leave feeling frustrated, giving me a look that seemed to say, *You liar.*

Within an hour of opening, the store sales total reached five thousand dollars—something I hadn't seen even at the end of a good sales day. People seemed possessed; it didn't look as if they had the need for any particular product, but were buying because they didn't want to miss out. We had extra-large bags—big enough to contain a human—that had been shipped to our store for this special day. People walked out, carrying the giant bags on their backs, staggering under the weight of discounted goods.

The hustle and bustle continued for a few hours, and by the time I got the chance to look at my watch, it was ten. The mayhem had abated to some extent. I looked around the store to assess the carnage. It looked like it had been looted—the wall that had been full of remote control cars a few hours ago had nothing on it now; aluminum shelves were bare; steel pegs were empty except for a lonely flashlight or laser key chain. The stacks of battery-operated helicopters that had been piled on the floor were gone, and the sales floor looked like it was covered with the remnants of a bomb explosion.

Black Friday in Charlottesville reminded me of Tuesdays in Lucknow. My mother and her mother used to visit a temple located in the middle of a historic shopping center in Lucknow. On Tuesdays, the temple organizes a worshipping ritual—a call-and-response chant known as *kirtan*—for Lord Hanuman, the monkey God. Hundreds of devotees, street urchins, beggars, and homeless people surround the temple while the priests sing, accompanied by loud drum beats and the deafening ring of gigantic, yellow-colored steel bells, echoing off every building in the vicinity. As the *kirtan* approaches its end, people outside the temple jostle to get close to the entrance; they want to get the biggest share of the *prasad*, the offering distributed in the form of sweets.

Not everyone manages to reach the holy offering, and those who do get it don't get a lot of it. Children pull on the sleeves of other children to stop them from getting a piece of *laddu*—a sugary round ball made of chickpea flour—and women balancing a child on their hips elbow out other women carrying a child. Sometimes two or three hands land at the same time on one tiny piece of *laddu*, pulling it in three different directions, causing it to get crushed and fall to the street in shards. Fights break out, creating a riot-like situation—quite like the ladies screaming at each other over the toy Rubicon in Charlottesville. While the torn pieces of packages, spilled coffee, and doughnut crumbs on the floor transported me to the temple scene in Lucknow, I heard Cindy call everyone for a quick get-together.

Watching people's enthusiasm about shopping on this day, I wondered what it was that motivated the United States of America to wake up at dawn to shop. If I had drunk and overeaten the night before, I would have loved to sleep in the next day. Waking up at four in the morning would be torture. I would not get in a line with a hundred people to buy something unless it was a bus ticket and I had to evacuate the city because a tornado was on its way.

Watching people walk by with bags crammed with stuff, I tried to understand their psyches. Maybe the corporations had brainwashed their minds into thinking that this was their one lucky day, the only day in the entire year to stock up. Maybe they had been waiting all year to buy that plasma TV or laptop.

Maybe it gave people some kind of thrill to see whether they could beat the crowd and be the one who seized the deal of the year. Maybe there were folks who treated this opportunity as some kind of an emotional therapy. I worked at ElectronicsHut and the entire store was available to me before it was to the customers. I could have bought anything and everything I wanted, but I didn't. I was, however, curious about what other stores had on sale. Maybe this day was about wanting whatever we didn't have, and not considering whatever we did have. I was thinking.

In the month after Black Friday, the mall was full of people walking around with three or four plastic bags that had different brand names on them. Everyone looked to be in a shopping stupor, as if this were what they had to do, whether they liked it or not. They would walk in and say, "D'you guys have that digital camera pack that comes with a printer, paper, and what not?"

"Yes, we do, sir!"

"Great, let me get three of those." They would not ask us to explain how it worked, what features it had, nor, most surprisingly, how much it cost. I would just grab it, scan the barcode, and put it in the bag. They would drop a thousand dollars like it was pocket change.

I noticed that women generally shopped during the day. They would spend a lot of time looking for something in different sections of the store, index finger on their chin, as if they were not sure what to get. I approached them and said, "Is there something I can help you with?"

"Yeah, I am trying to decide what to get for my twelve-year-old son. His dad has already bought him an iPod, but I don't know what I should get for him," a woman would say, looking at the display items on the shelf. I got used to this since there were a lot of moms trying to buy Christmas gifts for their twelve-, fourteen-, or sixteen-year-old children. I would often suggest to them some expensive gadget that they hadn't heard of before, and they would say, "Yeah, that sounds like an idea."

I would quickly grab it off the shelf before she took another minute to think, and just before I scanned it she would invariably say, "So, what is it supposed to do?" When I begin to explain the technical specifications—"It's a wireless FM transmitter for MP3 players, and"—she would interrupt me with, "Actually, you know what? I am technically challenged."

She would roll her eyes, and say, "My son will figure it out faster than me, let me just go ahead and get it."

I would take her money, and thank her for her business. She would then say, "Thank *you* for your help, I know I would have never found this thing—you have saved me so much time." According to hundreds of such women in Charlottesville, I saved them a lot of time over the course of one month. They came looking for a gift with a credit card ready in their hands. I suggested something they didn't know existed, and they paid for it appreciatively. I helped them save their time so that they could spend their money faster.

Men, on the other hand, came to shop only ten minutes before the store closed, and they didn't show up until a few days before Christmas. Oftentimes I didn't have to help them make up their minds. They came prepared. They would walk in, go straight to a particular product, pick it up, bring it to the counter, take the credit card out of their wallet, and hand it to me. It would take less than one minute, and one word—thanks!—to complete the transaction.

None of my colleagues had to try to sell anything to anyone. It seemed like the sales for this month of the year had been set into cruise control mode. None of us had to make an effort or do anything special or different to keep the customers rolling in. All we had to do was to stand behind the cash register, and people would continue to show up with something to buy. A normal day in this season saw at least eight thousand dollars worth of sales—sometimes much more.

The mall had extra kiosks—twice as many as any other time of the year—that were selling gift items: lotions, cheap Chinese-made toys, hats, picture frames. Christmas music played nonstop, and a large man dressed as Santa Claus walked around picking little kids up in his arms, saying "Ho ho ho." There were more lights in the mall than usual, and Christmas trees and wreaths adorned the entrances of every store.

Everyone seemed to be happy and in good spirits. It was the festive time of the year. Ben, the pretzel boy, didn't have to walk around the mall with a tray full of samples—people came to his store on their own. Justin, the barista, didn't have time to socialize because he had at least twenty people wanting to get coffee at any given minute. My Indian friends didn't seem to mind the rude customers since they were making good money, and they knew that they would be on a flight to India soon. For the first time in a long while, no one complained about business being slow.

CHAPTER TWENTY-ONE

Two Americas

Now that Holly and I were living in an apartment provided by the university, most people we got to know worked or studied at the University of Virginia. There, for the first time in Charlottesville, I got the chance to mingle with Indians. Most of them were doctoral students and postdoctoral fellows. A lot of them came from the Indian Institute of Technology, IIT, the prestigious institution for engineers in India. The kids who made it to IIT in India were from a different planet. At least that's how people who didn't make it there thought of them in India. Once admitted, they were treated with a god-like status. If you happened to bump into one of them, which was rare because they didn't usually socialize with people who weren't also IITians, they turned up their nose. In India, I knew a couple of people who went to IIT, but I had lost touch with them right after they got into the program. I had never imagined that I would play cricket with or hang out with a bunch IIT graduates on a regular basis, and that they would be the people I'd see on a regular basis in the United States. Living on the university campus, that is exactly what happened.

Although this unique situation gave me an opportunity to mingle with some of India's best minds, the same people became the bane of my existence. I was drawn to them because they looked like me and were brought up in the same culture and country, but I could never relate to them. Our childhoods had been very different. Growing up, they had had their noses buried in textbooks and homework. While they had been studying hard for exams, I had been playing cricket in the street. While they had been staying up all night to focus on algebra, I had been hanging out on the rooftop with my friends, joking and fooling around. With a strange stroke of luck, I found myself living next door to them in the United States. They were okay for the most part, but it irritated me hugely when they introduced me to a new friend of theirs.

"This is Deepak. His wife is a doctoral student. She is an American, but speaks fluent Hindi," they'd often say, in an effort to save me from the embarrassment of telling everyone that I was a salesman. They focused on my wife, not me. I gathered that the fact that I wasn't an engineer from a top institute in India was bad enough, but that I sold electronics in a retail store was much worse. They'd never consider a salesman to be their friend in India.

One day when I was at work I saw Ankit—an engineer friend of mine—walking past my store. He and I had become close over the last few months. He had grown up in a small town not too far from Lucknow. He always came to say hello to me at work when he came to the mall, which was often, but today he acted differently. He didn't stop. I waved at him from behind the counter to get his attention, but he acted like he hadn't seen me. I walked out of the store and stopped him. I saw he was with an older couple.

I remembered he had told me that his parents were going to visit him for a few weeks from India. He introduced me to them and I said *namaste* to his mother and father and they smiled at me. After a few pleasantries, they asked if I was also shopping in the mall, but before I could tell them that I actually worked there, my friend interrupted me. "Yes, mummy, he comes here a lot," he said. I looked at him, surprised. He immediately changed the subject. I got the feeling that he didn't want his parents to know that I worked in a store as a salesman. Ankit fidgeted and told me he was busy showing his folks around and that he would give me a call later. I felt like someone had punched me in the stomach. The humiliation of Ankit covering up for me was greater than the awkwardness of me admitting to his parents that I was a salesman.

I worked forty hours a week at the store. On my first day of work, Cindy had given me a sheet that looked like a chessboard. She'd asked me to fill out the hours of the day and days of the week that I was available to work. I had checked every box. I hadn't consulted with Holly before doing that. At the time, I didn't think I had any other agenda but to work. I had made myself available to work open to close, all days of the week. The only night I didn't work was Sunday, because the mall didn't stay open past 5:30 in the evening.

I always worked evenings and never took weekends off. Cindy liked that. She never wanted to work on the weekends, because she wanted to spend time with her kids. So did Ron and Jackie. I was the only one without a kid. But Holly didn't like it that I never tried to take weekends off. Her cohort in the anthropology department often held parties or happy hour get-togethers on the weekends. Holly and I were invited, but I couldn't go because

I had to work. I had gotten used to being around my colleagues at work. They had become my family and my friends in America. I shared stories and details of my life with them, saw them every day, went to eat out with them.

Sometimes, I went with her to the parties. One day, I got invited to a Super Bowl party. It was organized at one of Holly's friend's houses. Most of the people there were working on their PhDs in anthropology. Many of them were single, and the ones who were married brought along their spouses or partners. None of them were Indians, but some of them did research in India. Others worked in Tanzania, South Africa, Nepal, and China. Most of them were well traveled. They knew that India was in South Asia, not in the Middle East. They could distinguish between Hindu and Hindi, that one was a religion and the other a language. Some of them even knew where Lucknow was.

We got there a couple of hours before the game began. They began talking about how their work was going, how many years it was going to take before they finished their degree, how hard they were working on a grant application for a research trip to their respective fields. When they spoke of their research, they used a language that was not easily comprehensible. They talked like that, I assumed, to fit in, to prove to others that they belonged in the department and that they were smart. I usually never said anything. I didn't think I had anything to contribute.

I noticed that Holly spoke differently, too, when she spoke about her work.

"I am working on the role of infertility in crafting the idea of kinship in North India," she said. Her research was based in my hometown, and she had interviewed infertile women in Lucknow about what they thought about reproductive technologies, and about adopting a child. There was nothing I didn't understand about her research, but when she spoke to the anthropology folks about her work, I would look at her and wonder whether I actually understood her research.

I seemed to be constantly learning to talk to Americans. At work, there were my colleagues who never went to college, and then there were Holly and her friends who were tired of being in school. Their lives were worlds apart. My workmates often asked me what my wife did. When I told them she was working on her PhD in anthropology, they got quiet. It seemed like they didn't know what to ask or say. *University, anthropology, PhD*— those words seemed like something from a different planet to them.

Back in India, when I was still finishing my MBA, I often took an auto-rickshaw to go to college. One day, a rickshaw driver named Bablu asked me what I was studying. When I told him, he gave me a blank look.

"What is the meaning of this?"

"I am learning how to manage a business."

He then asked me how much it cost. I told him. He got quiet again, and then after a pause, he said, "If I had this much money, I could buy ten cows and start a milk dairy in my village."

I had laughed, paid him the fare, and walked into my school building. I thought I could use his example in one of my case studies. I felt sorry for him and thought about coming up with a business plan to help people like Bablu. I thanked my stars for not being a Bablu myself.

In America, I was a Bablu of sorts. I'd often wake up in the middle of the night, hallucinating, dreaming about where I had come from and where I was going. It didn't help that our apartment was right on Route 29, the main artery of Charlottesville.

The sounds of police sirens and fire trucks throughout the night were commonplace. Next to our apartment was the Econo Lodge. Its neon red sign illuminated our bedroom. If we put the blinds down to avoid the red light, it reappeared as red-hot iron rods on the wall, making the bedroom look like an interrogation chamber. We couldn't escape it.

Startled by a bad dream, I'd get up and go to the living room. I would sit on the futon and look around our apartment, running my eyes across everything we owned. The square dining table in the right corner of the room, near the window, which one of Holly's friends had given her when we moved in, a leftover from her own childhood. The futon from another friend of hers. Two wooden chairs. An old recliner from the same friend who'd given the table. An Ikea desk, and on top of it an old black laptop that Holly and I shared. A couple of bookshelves for our books, and some wall hangings that Holly and I had brought back from India. The most expensive thing we had was a car, a large used Oldsmobile, but we hadn't bought it. It came from Holly's grandparents.

Holly was still quite a few years away from finishing her PhD, and I wasn't getting any response to the applications I was making for salaried jobs at the university. I thought about going back to school, though I wasn't sure exactly what I'd study. Holly didn't think that was a good idea. She didn't think we could both afford to be students at the same time. The other option was to get better at what I was doing, selling electronics, and become a manager of the store. I was getting better at my job, but I wasn't sure whether that was what I wanted to continue doing. I knew how hard my manager worked, much longer hours than me, and how much more she was responsible for. I didn't think I could be anywhere as confident as her in handling irate customers, training new employees, and keeping up with the massive amounts of paperwork. Most nights I went to bed worrying.

About six months after I had arrived in the United States, my father had been diagnosed with a heart condition. He had several blocked arteries. The doctors had advised him to have bypass surgery, but he was very scared. He avoided it for a year, but the doctors kept telling him that he was taking a great risk in doing that. He couldn't walk too far without having pain in his chest. He had to stop several times to cover a small distance. My mother worried about his health a lot. I was away and when my younger brother moved to New Delhi to get his MBA, my parents became quite lonely.

As the eldest son, I felt guilty for moving to America. I worried about my father's health a lot, so much that I slowly became convinced that I, too, had a heart problem, a blocked artery. I kept this to myself and didn't reveal it to Holly, but I looked for symptoms like chest pain, or pain in my left arm. If I strained a muscle in my shoulder, I would attribute it to the possible blocked artery in my heart. When I climbed up a flight of stairs and ran out of breath, I'd have the sinking feeling that my heart was going bad. It kept getting worse. Every once in a while, when I found out a customer was a heart specialist, a cardiac surgeon, I would tell him that I thought I had a heart condition. Some of them laughed at me and said, "No, don't worry. There are too many things that can cause chest pain. You are too young to have a heart problem." Some others would say, "You should get yourself checked out. Don't take a chance."

I was too scared to go to a doctor. I worried that he would tell me to get bypass surgery. The thought that my father and I, both of us, might have to go under the knife gave me nightmares. A time came when I couldn't take it any more and told Holly about what was going on inside my head. She didn't pay much attention to it in the beginning. But I wasn't joking about the trauma it was causing me. I worried about it so much that I stopped smiling. Every time I heard about someone having a heart attack, I knew that mine was coming. I would be woken in the night by sounds of an ambulance or fire truck. Holly would touch my chest to see whether my heart was racing too fast.

No matter how rough my night had been, I would have to drag myself out of bed, iron my shirt and pants, take a shower, put my clothes and smile on, and show up at work.

CHAPTER TWENTY-TWO

Paula

Paula, one of the golden-quarter seasonal employees, was no taller than five feet, and young. Her wavy blonde hair reached her waist when she didn't have it tied up in a bun. She had a lot of energy packed in her little body; she rarely stayed in one place for more than a minute, and if she did, she would shift her feet and move her shoulders to keep time with the music in the store. A garrulous person, she wasn't shy about saying anything to anyone. Since she had worked as a waitress in all her previous jobs, making conversation came to her naturally. I could imagine her being a great waitress.

One day when she and I were working together, she asked me, "Is your wife white?"

"She is, why?" I asked, wondering what had brought on the question.

"No, I think I saw her one day when she came to pick you up. I wasn't sure if she was really your wife."

"Yes, she is my wife," I said.

"Do people look at you strangely when you are with her?" she asked.

"What do you mean?" I asked.

"You know, I have a child with an African American man, so I'm cool with interracial relationships," she said, "but some people don't like it."

"I am sure there are people who give me strange looks," I said.

"You have any kids?" she asked, with a sparkle in her eyes.

"Not yet."

"I've got two."

"Okay."

"One's two years old and the other one is six months," she said. "My boyfriend is going to bring them here in a few minutes."

"Okay," I said. I wondered about her age because she didn't look old enough to have two kids.

A few minutes later a young man walked into the store with two babies, one in a stroller and another in a sling wrapped around his chest. He had oil spots all over his clothes and boots. His face and hands were smudged with grease, and the edges of his nails were black.

"There he is," Paula said, and ran towards the man. As she reached him, she stood up on her toes trying to give an extra inch to her height, and lifted her face up. Her boyfriend bent down a few inches to bring himself down to her level, shifted the baby in the sling onto one side, and planted a kiss on her lips.

"Why are you so tall, babe?" she said.

"I'm not tall, you're just too short," the guy replied.

"Deepak, this is Eli, my boyfriend," she slapped his shoulder, and said, "and these are my babies." I shook hands with Eli, and introduced myself. Paula and Eli talked for a few minutes, played with their babies, and then kissed each other goodbye. "Eli is a car mechanic. He knows everything about cars and he can take apart any car and put it back together. He's real smart," Paula said.

"Great," I said, and looked at her as she continued talking.

"You know, Eli is a nice guy, and he's good with my kids even though one of them is not his."

"That's good," I said, feeling amazed at Paula's willingness to volunteer information.

"You know, I like this job, it's fast paced and all, but I liked my last job better."

"Why did you leave it then?"

"Well—" she looked at me, biting the inside of her cheeks. "You really wanna know?"

"Yeah, if you don't mind telling," I said.

"The reason why I liked my last job was because my boss didn't mind me coming in late, or taking a day off here and there."

"Why didn't he mind you coming in late to work?"

She looked to her right and to her left, and said in a hushed voice, "It's because I used to have sex with him every once in a while." I didn't know what to say. I wasn't expecting to know about Paula's sex life.

"I wasn't with Eli then," she said, "but I don't like to hide anything. I told him about it when we started dating."

"What did he think about it?"

"Eli thought it was gross," she said, and shrugged her shoulders. "But hey, my boss let me come in late, and I got away with easy schedules and things like that, you know."

"So, were you actually dating your boss?" I asked.

"Oh, no, no, no. We both would've lost of our jobs if we had gotten into a formal relationship," she said. "It was just a no-strings-attached thing." I became curious and wondered where and how the two of them could have met. While I was still trying to think of a polite way to inquire, she said, "It just used to be a quickie in the bathroom or the kitchen."

"No," I said, trying to process what I had just heard.

"Hey, you know what?" she said. I looked at her, and prepared myself for whatever she was going to tell me next.

"Tomorrow is my birthday!" she said, and took a spin, balancing on her heels. "I am turning twenty-one."

"What are you going to do for your twenty-first birthday?" I asked.

"Get drunk. Oh, yes!" Customers interrupted our conversation, but every time there was a quiet period, Paula talked. She told me that she was living with her grandmother because it was cheaper than renting her own place. She said that she wasn't enjoying being a salesperson because it didn't provide her the kind of environment she was used to. She loved being a waitress because it gave her a chance to chat with people, entertain them, and get free food. She liked going to parties, and loved dancing. She mentioned that she wouldn't mind being a stay-at-home mom if her husband were rich, but she had to work because she owed a lot of money to the hospital because of the delivery of her two sons. Paula's life was very different from that of every twenty-year-old girl I had known in India.

It was 1989, and I was in tenth grade. For the first time in my life, I was going to be formally taught about sex. In my biology class we were going to begin the chapter on reproduction. It was a chapter every boy in my class looked forward to, not only because they were eager to learn about sex, but also because they were curious to see how Ms. Khosla, a young teacher in her mid-twenties, handled thirty-odd boys.

The chapter had plenty of diagrams—penis, uterus, fetus, mammary glands, and vagina. Those few pages in the book were like a porn magazine for my rowdy friends in the back row of the classroom. We had zero access to real porn magazines. It was scandalous to buy one, and even if we had managed to get our hands on one, there would have been no way to bring a magazine with nude pictures into our homes. A biology course book with diagrams of human organs was as close as we got. Even with a required book for school, I used to be careful not to look at those images too closely in the presence of my parents. If they caught me reading the chapter, they would give me a look, a look that was just as bad as getting caught masturbating.

But in the school, sitting in the very back of the classroom, we looked through the pages, running our fingers on the female genitalia, no matter what class we were in—physics, mathematics, English, Hindi, history, or geography.

I went to a coed school. There were just as many girls in my class as boys, but we didn't mingle much. There were two rows of desks, and although there was no said rule, girls chose to sit in one row and boys in another. We were together, but segregated. We had school uniforms. Boys wore white shirts and dark-blue pants. Girls wore monogrammed white shirts tucked into knee-length dark-blue skirts. *Dupattas,* scarfs, were not allowed for girls in school, which made them uncomfortable. The school principal was very strict and made sure the kids behaved, but there was no way of keeping the boys from checking out breasts. Girls couldn't report to the teacher that boys always kept their eyes focused a few inches below their chins. When boys talked with girls, the discussions were almost always about homework, school, or something to with the lessons. There was no casual talk.

On the day Ms. Khosla was supposed to teach the chapter on reproduction, there was a strange silence in the class. She walked in wearing a bright yellow sari and red lipstick, with her hair in a bun. Ms. Khosla was quite fashionable and liked to wear long colorful sleeveless shirts with loose pants, but this was different. She never wore a sari to school. We almost didn't recognize her. Everyone stood up, like always, to welcome the teacher into the class. Then we sat down. Girls fidgeted in their seats, fixing their shirts, their ponytails. Boys looked attentive. It was the last period, the last lesson of the school day. Usually by this time, the students were worn out. But not today.

Ms. Khosla furtively scanned the class, as if to see the mood. A lot of times, she had to remind us to read the chapter before- hand. Today was different. Each one of us, at least all my friends, had read the chapter so many times that they could recite each word of it without looking at the book. Ms. Khosla cleared her throat—a sign she wasn't sure how to begin. She stole a look at her wristwatch from the corner of her eyes. We had thirty-two minutes before school was over. Everyone was silent, so silent you could hear a pin drop.

The awkwardness was not unlike the uneasiness when my fam- ily watched TV together and a condom ad popped up. My parents had recently bought a black-and-white television. It was housed in a rectangular dark-brown wooden cabinet and it occupied a lot of space in our tiny bedroom. My whole family watched the shows together, and when we didn't, the television was turned off—shut- ters drawn, an embroidered cloth hanging over it. There were only two channels and both were government-owned. Lately, there had been a lot of advertisements about condoms on TV. Every time an advert about condoms popped up, my parents and my sister didn't know what to say. My younger brother was seven and sometimes he asked, "What's Pleasure, mummy?" We kept staring at the screen without uttering a word, feigning complete ignorance. No one smiled. No one fidgeted. We didn't stand up or move. We couldn't get angry at his question, or express our amusement. We just waited for the ad to end. Thirty seconds became three hours.

Ms. Khosla seemed like a model in a TV advertisement. Students were the audience. After a few minutes, she asked us to begin reading the chapter aloud, one student at a time. We didn't want this. We had already read it, and we got the feeling that this was our teacher's strategy to shift the focus away from her. We had a lot of questions that we would have liked her to answer. We'd read the chapter, but not everything was clear to us. Ms. Khosla was the only person who could explain it to us. For people like me, who were going to pick a nonscience subject in eleventh grade, this was the first and last sex education class. But, we couldn't protest, or even ask her a question that day.

Each one of us read one paragraph. Girls read so softly we could barely hear. Boys couldn't read without snorting. Soon the bell rang. Ms. Khosla told us to read the rest of the chapter at home. She gave the questions at the back of the chapter for homework. The wait for our chance to learn about sex came to an abrupt end. I graduated from high school and then college, but never had a formal education or counseling about sex and relationships. And then I got a job where a major part of my duties involved educating others about sex.

Soon after I finished my MBA, a friend of a friend introduced me to a BBC producer, a British Asian who spoke almost no Hindi, in

Lucknow. Impressed with my English language skills, he offered me a position in his team, which was responsible for producing radio shows for the BBC. The hour-long weekly show aired across the northern state of Uttar Pradesh, the biggest state in India by population, with close to two hundred million residents. The point of the show was to spread awareness about HIV. The biggest challenge for the production team was to figure out how to talk about sex on the show without talking about sex. We wanted people to listen to the show, not to get disgusted or offended and turn off their radios. We spent months on workshops, brainstorming sessions, discussions, and meetings with the state health ministers, executives from health departments, and radio producers from the BBC. There was one common goal: to educate Indians about HIV prevention, especially safe sex, without hurting sensitivities.

I was part of the BBC team that was responsible for starting the show from the ground up. Before the first show aired, we had to hire two presenters who were comfortable with the theme of the show. When we took out the advertisement in the *Times of India*, we said we were looking for two presenters for a radio show about HIV awareness, but we didn't give too many details. Many candidates showed up for mock on-air auditions. We asked them to explain sexual intercourse. We were looking for people who could explain correctly, but in the most indirect way. The presenter's job didn't really involve describing the actual act on the radio, but we wanted to see how well they would handle a difficult subject like this. We spent an entire day in the studio interviewing dozens of people. Every single woman who showed up for the job left immediately after learning what the show was about. Most men stayed for the interview, but all of them fared badly. Some were very childish, some were crude, and some couldn't stop giggling.

Disappointed, we finally decided to pick one young man who had done a moderately good job. Now we had to find a woman to be his co-host. We liked one presenter who was already working at a different radio station. She was a local celebrity and had a very good rapport with her audience. We thought it would be easier for the audience to listen in and pay attention to a trusted presenter. We got in touch with her. She was willing to talk to us. When she learned about what she would have to do on the show, she refused, flatly. We offered her twice the money she was making at the other place.

"I won't do it," she replied, "even if you pay me four times as much." We were disheartened, but we understood why she didn't want to work for us. Things might have been different in cosmopolitan cities like Mumbai and Delhi, but it was almost unheard of for women or girls to talk about sex in public in most of India, and certainly in Lucknow. Finally, we found a presenter through word of mouth. She was from Lucknow, but had traveled around the world and was open-minded. But writing the script for the show was always tricky. We worried about protests against the show if we went too far across cultural lines. Even in the early 2000s, it was a bit of a daring move to make a show like this. Sex was a taboo subject, especially for women. Everyone was curious about it, but talking about it wasn't easy.

Growing up in India, I had some idea that American women were open about their sexuality, and that talking about sex was not a taboo in America. But this was the first time that someone had narrated such intimate details of her private life to me. Listening to Paula openly talk about sex made me realize how different our upbringings had been, and how different our worlds were. Paula knew very little about my cultural background. I wondered how she would react if I told her that in my country it would be a huge scandal if a colleague were to discuss her sex life with me.

She was now done helping a customer. As soon as the person left the store she looked at me and said, "Deepak, you know what else I'm going to do for my twenty-first birthday?

I looked at her, curious.

"Get my belly button pierced," she said with a grin.

CHAPTER TWENTY-THREE

Cameron

Paula soon quit. She had found a job closer to where she lived. She said it was easier to manage with her kids. After she left, Cindy scheduled me to work with Cameron. Unlike Paula, he was very quiet. Most of his answers were nods or shrugs. He was skinny and short, and had shoulder-length hair braided into many strands with beads tied to them. He talked and moved slowly. He appeared to have no interest in learning the inventory or doing well at sales. He would often lean on the counter with his hands behind his back, while resting his gaze on something in the store, or outside it. It seemed like he was lost in his own thoughts.

Ron, Jackie, and I were generally eager to outdo each other. We tried to get an advantage by attracting a customer's attention first. We sometimes hung around the entrance to grab a new customer as soon as she walked in. While everyone tried to sell and make commissions, Cameron would stand around the counter and watch TV. He mostly stayed behind and helped customers only when no one else was around to do it.

This annoyed Cindy, since she was the one who had originally thought he should be given a chance. She wondered why he didn't take the initiative and walk up to customers, but would instead spend a long time talking to them *after* someone else had made the sale. Oftentimes, the customer would be on her way out with her purchase, and only then would Cameron engage her in a long conversation. He talked with people in a manner that suggested he was conspiring, cutting a secret deal, or discussing a plot. Something seemed odd about it. The customers didn't seem to mind that he stood very close to them and spoke in a hushed voice. They listened to him carefully while he talked two inches away from them.

"Why would you wanna spend so much time with someone who's leaving the store after buying a teeny-weeny battery pack?" Cindy would say under her breath and shake her head.

After a few days of Cameron being at work, we noticed something interesting. Some of the same people he was chatting with would return after a few hours, the next day, or even a few days later. They would come back looking for Cameron. If Cameron wasn't there, they refused to talk to anyone else, and asked when they could talk to him. This seemed strange since the people he had talked with had been originally helped by someone else in the store—Ron, Jackie, or me—but they would not ask for any of us.

He surprised everyone with his sales numbers in our next meeting. He was the top seller. Nobody could believe it. He never seemed to sell anything and spent most of the time standing behind the counter, staring at the television. I was curious and pulled out the sales sheet for the last two weeks. He had only a few tickets, but he had sold top-dollar merchandise—a flat plasma TV, a projector, a laptop, stuff like that.

Cameron began to intrigue everybody. Some days he didn't sell more than a hundred dollars' worth of merchandise, but he never got angry or frustrated. His face never seemed to show any emotion. I was amazed to see a twenty-year-old display so much patience. I wanted to know why his sales total on some days didn't even reach a hundred dollars, but on other days he could sell expensive items worth a thousand dollars.

He must be doing something right, I thought. I started paying attention when Cameron talked with a customer. In his approach to customers, I noticed he had something that was unique: his level of tenacity.

I talked to the customers, tried to understand what they wanted, explained the features of the product, gave them enough time to make a decision, and considered myself good at being courteous and not pressuring them into buying. But watching Cameron deal with a customer made me think that I was a truly impatient man. He would spend more than an hour, sometimes two hours, talking to a customer. While the person stared at a particular product, Cameron would stand right next to him the whole time like a shadow. Also, he wouldn't say much—he let the customer do most of the talking.

Cindy, Ron, and Jackie never did that—it was an unofficial rule not to spend too long with just one customer. Cameron's technique had both pluses and minuses. He was missing out on other customers while he concentrated on just one. The effective thing was that his spending half the day with a customer made the person feel guilty if she didn't buy something. It wasn't often that customers were so unsure that they needed a salesperson to spend four hours with them to help them decide what they wanted to buy. When someone of that nature happened to walk in our store, Cameron had an unerring ability to recognize the type, and claim him or her.

Anytime it was slow, I tried to have a conversation with him. He was quiet and introverted, but he didn't mind me talking to him. I got the feeling that he liked my company. One day when he was staring at nothing, like he always did, I asked him, "Do you like working here?"

"It's awright," he said, without looking at me. There was no emotion in his voice. He made it sound like I had asked him about the taste of a drink that he was having—it was no big deal to him—he could take it or leave it. There was no telling from his tone if he hated the job, liked it, or was just whiling his time away. I couldn't decide what to say or ask next. After a long silence he said, "I can't take no risks no more."

Not understanding what he meant, I said, "Risks? What do you mean?"

"I got two kids. One is three years old and the other one just turned one. I can't afford to go to jail no more, y'know what I mean?" This one sentence revealed many things that I wasn't expecting to hear from a twenty-year-old. What did he mean by taking risks? How come he had two kids when he himself was still a kid? What did he mean he couldn't afford to go to jail anymore?

I didn't know what to say except to wait for him to speak more. We noticed a couple hovering around the MP3 player section. He rolled up his sleeves, revealing his dark, skinny arms, and walked toward them. While he talked to the people, I stood there wondering about what he had said. When he had finished with the couple, it was time to close.

Cindy started scheduling me with Cameron often. To ease myself into a conversation, I told him a little about myself—

where I was from, how long I had been at the job, and how I liked it. I didn't want him to feel I was being too nosy. After a few minutes, he asked me, "You got any kids, Deepak?"

"No, not yet."

"Alright."

"How old were you when you had your first kid?"

"Young, very young—sixteen, I had just turned sixteen," he said. The only other person I knew who had had a child at age sixteen was my grandmother. That was in the 1930s in a backward village in North India. She was not educated and had been married at the age of fourteen. It was strange to hear a twenty-year-old telling me he was the father of two kids.

At age sixteen, I was fooling around, flying kites, playing marbles in the alleys, spinning tops in stairwells, throwing little rocks from the top of the roof at people walking in the street below, joking.

"How did it feel to be a dad at age sixteen?" I asked him.

He looked at me, sucked his lips, and shrugged his shoulders. A few seconds later he said, "One day my girlfriend told me she was pregnant. I didn't know what to do. We were still in school and there was no way I could support her, or raise a kid."

"What did you do then?"

"I went home and told my momma that my girlfriend was pregnant." I continued looking at him, briefly glancing at the entrance to see if anyone was coming. "My mom is a janitor and works long hours. She's a tough woman. She's gone through a lot in life."

"What did she say when you gave her the news?"

"She said that I'd have to grow up to be a man now, and be responsible," he said, looking outside. I kept quiet. "Yep. That's what she told me," he said, nodding his head in slow motion. I was eager to know how a sixteen-year-old boy handled having a baby at an age when he should have been studying.

"I dropped out of school and took a job." Watching me listening to him intently, he said, "Yep, that's what I did," and took a deep breath. "I've been working ever since then, Deepak."

Over the course of the next few days, Cameron and I got to work together a few more times. He later told me he had had another kid with the same young woman, but broke up with her soon after that. He often called her from work to talk to his kids.

He would step aside and say things like, "You know Daddy loves you, Daddy loves you. I love you." His eyes would become moist after these phone conversations. "I miss my kids, Deepak," he would tell me. He said he was dating another woman who had a child with someone else. She visited him in the store sometimes.

One day, when I closed the store with Cameron, I asked him if he could give me a ride home. He said, "Of course, Deepak." We clocked out and walked out. My eyes scanned the parking lot for an old, beat-up, cheap vehicle, assuming that would be what Cameron would be able to afford. He walked toward the center of the lot, where there were two cars parked. One was very old, had paint peeling off the side bumper, and tires that had no tread. The other was a long, white, swank Cadillac. I approached the older car and stood by the passenger side, waiting for him to come around to the driver's seat.

The Cadillac's lights flashed. I thought the owner of the car must have turned on the lights as he approached. Then I heard a friendly honk. I looked around for Cameron ... and saw him in the Cadillac, honking at me to get inside.

He had the passenger door open for me. I slid myself into the leather seat, which was already warm from the built-in heating system. I shut the door, and put the seat belt on. I had never been inside a Cadillac. It was unsettling. Riding home, my bottom cradled in a warm leather seat that was more comfortable than any chair I could remember, listening to music that did not seem to be coming out of car speakers but made me think I was in an opera house, and riding along so effortlessly that I forgot the asphalt was there, I felt like I was gliding on the surface of smooth waters.

When we arrived at my house, I asked, "So, how did you end up with a Cadillac?"

He said, "It's a leftover from my drug-selling days, Deepak."

He backed the car out, gave me another friendly honk, and drove away. I climbed the stairs to my apartment, thinking about what he meant when he said he couldn't afford to take any more risks, or go to jail. I went to bed thinking that twenty-year-old Cameron had gone through a lot—babies, breakups, drugs, and more.

The next day when I went to work, Cindy told me Cameron wouldn't be working with us anymore. She didn't know the reason, but she didn't seem surprised. I never got to ride in that Cadillac again.

It's been several years since then, but I often think of Cameron.

CHAPTER TWENTY-FOUR

Don't Sue Me!

As a young kid I often used stomachaches as an excuse to avoid going to school. My parents could never tell if my tummy was really hurting or I was just faking; teachers didn't ask for a doctor's note, since stomachaches weren't the kind of illness that required a visit to the hospital. In my case, I usually got better by two in the afternoon—around the time school got out. It was a handy problem to come up with when I didn't feel like spending eight hours in a classroom. My mother always suspected that it was just an excuse and for that reason she would look at my face to detect the fakery. She would say things like, "What did you eat yesterday? I don't think I cooked anything that could cause a stomach upset. Everyone else seems to be okay."

Since I knew my acting would be put to the test, I would grab my tummy, bend in two, shove my face into the pillow, and not look up for a very long time. She would give up, and say, "You never seem to get sick on a Sunday for some reason." I would lift my head just enough to breathe and sneak a look to see if she was still there. Seeing her long shadow created by the rising sun,

I would duck my head back into the pillow, bending and twisting my torso. Stomachache stories continued into my adulthood. Schoolteachers, college professors, tutors, bosses—everyone got to hear one. Some of my friends teased me. "Oh, Deepak's here, seems like his stomach's not hurting today."

One day in Charlottesville, I didn't feel like going to work. It was a beautiful day, and I just didn't want to spend my time inside a building surrounded by electronics. I took the phone inside the bathroom, sat on the toilet seat, and called Cindy. I left a message on her answering machine saying that I was sick, and brought the phone close as I flushed the toilet. I thought the sound of water running would give me some credibility since I hadn't actually talked to her, and she didn't get to listen to my weary voice.

I enjoyed not working. The next day, I showed up wearing neatly ironed clothes, my hair well combed, looking fresh. As soon as I walked in, Cindy came to me, looking worried.

"Are you okay, Deepak?" she asked.

Surprised by her concern, I said, "Yeah," trying to figure out what made her ask that. Taking a healthy stride forward, I moved toward the backroom.

Jackie, who was cutting open a box, stopped and said, "You feelin' alright Deepak?"

"Yes, I am," I said matter-of-factly.

"What made you sick?" It dawned on me that I had totally forgotten that I had been off the day before, and was supposed to have been out sick. Since my days off were mostly during the week—and because I had never called in sick before—I had confused my sick day with a regular day off. I realized I was supposed to look tired, weak, and disheveled.

I had to come up with a quick answer to Jackie's question. I said, "Oh, I think I ate something in the mall and that might have made me sick." As soon as I finished the sentence, I realized that she might find it hard to believe since I always brought lunch from home.

"For real?" she asked. Before I tried to explain more, she said, "Where did you eat?" Glad to be past the first hurdle, I said, "I think I ate at that pizza place." I thought she wouldn't ask any more questions and would leave me alone, but I didn't realize that by telling her where I had eaten, I'd gotten myself into bigger trouble.

I'd never had such an interrogation in India. You knew that people knew that you were lying. There, I didn't have to act like I was sick, and no one asked any questions about what made me sick since they already knew that I wasn't sick. Stomachaches were "don't-ask-don't-tell" kinds of excuses.

I hung my coat, and started walking away from Jackie. "Oh, you know what Deepak? You should go sue them," she said just when I was stepping out of the backroom. I took a step back, and looked at her. She didn't look like she was joking.

I smiled, and said, "Sue them for what?"

She said, "Sue them because their food made you sick. They will pay for your medicines, hospital bills, and whatever—" I had never had to visit a lawyer, and had never sued anyone in my life. Hearing Jackie talk with such seriousness, I didn't know how to react. I wanted to laugh out loud.

I said, "Yes, you are right, Jackie, but it's okay. I won't eat there again."

"No, Deepak, I am serious, you should go sue them." She dropped the box cutter, and walked onto the sales floor. "Cindy, I think Deepak should sue those pizza people—he ate there the other day and got sick."

"Hey, you know what?" Cindy turned around, and said, "my stomach has been feeling weird since I ate their pizza the other day." This was getting out of control. I knew I hadn't eaten there, and I was not sick. I didn't want to sue anyone, and especially not for something that never happened. Cindy walked hurriedly to the backroom.

She came back in a flash, and said, "Deepak, let's go and talk to those people." A court scene flashed in my mind—me standing inside a wooden box facing the pizza guy, the judge telling me that they couldn't find any evidence that I had eaten the pizza, and then fining me hundreds of dollars for lying.

Terrified by just thinking of what could happen, I told Cindy, "I am sorry, Cindy, but I don't want to do this."

"Why?"

"It's because I am not 100 percent sure that it was the pizza that made me sick."

"Alright, that's fair enough." I fixed my collar and walked back to the backroom to get a glass of water. I had never thought that calling in sick could cause such a drama. I also didn't know that people were ready to take anyone to court for trivial matters such as getting sick from eating pizza.

In India, I could never imagine suing a roadside street vendor who sold samosas—fried dumplings—to hundreds of people. The thought of taking the vendor to court would not occur to anyone, even if he or she knew for sure that it was the vendor's food that had caused a serious stomach infection. The most they would do is not eat there again. Hiring a lawyer would require too much effort, time and money, and God only knows what they would get if they won the lawsuit—maybe a free meal if they were lucky.

The saga of suing the pizza guy brought to mind an incident that took place in Chowk—an older part of Lucknow. I was with my friends, eating at a famous kebab place that served tiny round meat patties with flat bread. Everything was being cooked right before our eyes. We were enjoying the food and admiring the high ceilings. The restaurant building seemed to be very old. We finished eating, and just when we were leaving the place, I asked the manager, who was sitting at the entrance, "How old is this building?"

Dabbing a thumb on his tongue to help count the rupees, he said, "Hundred and eighty years old."

I said, "Wow, the owner must be a rich man."

He said, "Not really." He pointed his finger at someone wearing tattered clothes, sitting at the curb on the street, smoking a *bidi,* tobacco wrapped in a leaf. "That's the owner," he said. I was surprised, and wanted to ask more about him, but the manager wasn't in the mood to answer any more questions.

I came out of the restaurant, and stood next to the person who was supposed to be the owner. I looked at him. He looked at me. He appeared frail and old. Gray hairs were peeking out of his shirt, which revealed his scrawny chest. His teeth were stained from too much smoking. I made it clear that I wanted to talk to him. I said, "I've been told you are the owner of that building."

"Yes, I am," he said.

"The building must be worth a lot of money, isn't it?"

"It is."

"So—"

"Are you wondering why I am sitting here smoking a *bidi?*"

"Yes," I said, and smiled.

He pointed his finger in one direction and said, "All these shops in this building are owned by people like me. You can find them sleeping on the steps of the building, on the sidewalk, or in the liquor store drinking cheap country-made alcohol."

"So, what am I missing here?" I said. "Why are they in such a state?"

"My ancestors rented this building to the ancestors of that kebab guy. The terms of contract haven't changed in the last hundred years, and the rent is still thirty rupees—fifty cents—a month. I have taken the matter to court, but it's been thirty years, and who knows how long it will take." He scratched his stubble, and looked at me helplessly. "I hang around this building because I know I own it, but all I get is thirty rupees from him. He is the one who is making money, using my property. I can't do anything."

Thirty rupees might have been a big sum as a monthly rent one hundred years ago, but now it wouldn't even get me a plate full of kebabs in Lucknow. When Jackie wanted me to sue the pizza place in Charlottesville, I couldn't help but think about that poor owner of the building sitting outside the restaurant, smoking cheap *bidis*.

After a week or two, when people at work had forgotten about me getting sick, I told Cindy how my friends in India would laugh if they found out that I wanted to sue someone for selling a bad pizza.

"Why?"

"It's because people don't go to court for something as minor as getting sick from eating at a restaurant."

"Really?"

"Yes."

"In this country people are always scared about getting sued for something or other," she said. She paused for a moment, and said, "See that yellow sign there? The mall has to put it out every time they mop the floors, because if people slip and get hurt they could sue the mall for not warning them." I had seen the sign before, and I knew it was supposed to tell people that the floor was wet, but I didn't know that people could actually sue the mall if the sign wasn't there and they slipped and got hurt.

"So, people would sue even if it was their own fault that they fell?" I asked.

"Oh yeah, people are always looking for an excuse to sue you," said Cindy. "They would sue a coffee shop for not warning them that the coffee was too hot to drink, they would sue an ice cream place for serving them too cold an ice cream, they would sue a barber for giving them a bad haircut, and they would sue you for the most ridiculous thing you could ever think of. And you can get in some serious trouble if you get sued. Some people have gone bankrupt, spent a long time in jail, you know."

After Cindy told me how Americans were always ready to sue, I realized that most businesses in the mall took steps to protect themselves from being sued. I started noticing warning signs on everything. I had never paid attention to the coffee I got from Justin, but when I looked, I saw that the lid of the cup said, in capital letters, "CAUTION HOT." A clearly wet floor had a sign that said "WET FLOOR." A cookie shop that sold cookies with nuts in them had a sign that said "WARNING: OUR COOKIES CONTAIN NUTS." A door that opened automatically when you approached had one that said "CAUTION: AUTOMATIC DOOR."

The culture of cautioning people about every little thing seemed a little overdone. Having grown up in a country where such warnings were not common, I had gotten used to surprises. I once found an antenna-type thing sticking out of my teacup, which turned out to be a spider leg. I complained to the tea guy; he threw the rest of the tea and the spider away, filled the cup up again, and gave it to me as if it were no big deal. Another time, my mother sent me to get a spice that was supposed to go in a dish she was cooking. The grocery store was down the road, next to a bicycle repair shack. I walked down wearing my bathroom slippers. As I was dealing with the shopkeeper, I felt as if my big toe were on fire. I looked down and saw a welding gun spitting blue flame right next to my foot. The bicycle guy next door had turned the machine on without realizing where the gun was. I came home hopping on one leg with no spice.

Yet another time, when I was riding on my bicycle, singing a happy Hindi song, I fell into an open manhole that had no warning around it. Luckily the bicycle wheel was too big to go through the hole. I managed to stay above ground. All these incidents taught me that if anything bad happened to me, it had to be entirely my fault. I must not have looked, or I should have been more careful. No one suggested suing the *chaiwallah* for serving tea with spiders in it, the bicycle-repair guy for being careless with his welding torch, or the municipal corporation of Lucknow for leaving the manhole open.

A few days later, on a Sunday, I was supposed to work at the store by myself; the other scheduled employee called in sick. Sundays were short days since the mall was open for just five hours. I could have handled it on my own, but Cindy arranged for Alexi, an employee from a different store, to come assist me for a few hours.

It was a usual Sunday—families dressed in nice clothes coming after church to have lunch in the mall, husbands and wives walking hand in hand enjoying a day off, casually strolling, and checking out the deals in various stores. Normally, we didn't do a lot of business on Sundays; since people knew we were only open for five hours, most of them didn't bother coming in. Once in a while we got busy, but it was mostly slow.

In the last hour, I saw a lady walking in with a digital camera bundle pack. This was bad news since it was already a slow day, and if she returned the camera—which was worth about four hundred dollars—it would put the total sales for the day in the negative. She was a middle-aged white lady with short hair, wearing a light-green T-shirt and white shorts. She took hurried steps, and brought the camera box to the counter and put it in front of Alexi.

"Just need to return it. My husband bought this for me a few days ago, but I don't need it," she said, and pulled a crumpled receipt from her purse. Alexi looked at the receipt, and showed it to me. The camera had been bought only two weeks ago, so it was within the time frame of our return policy. I had been hoping she had bought it more than a month ago so we could just do an exchange and not return the money. I looked at Alexi, and she looked at me. We didn't say anything, but we understood what we wanted to say—*it sucks!* Alexi started to refund the sale, but when she looked for the barcode on the camera package, she noticed that it had been cut out—there was a hole instead.

Alexi showed it to me, and I immediately knew what had happened. About fifteen days ago we had run a mail-in-rebate sale on the cameras. Customers were supposed to pay four hundred dollars for the camera, but they could get a hundred dollars back if they filled out the information on the receipt, and sent it in along with the barcode on the package. This lady seemed to have taken advantage of the rebate before she brought the camera to the store. I asked her where the barcode was, since we couldn't take the product back without it.

She seemed prepared for the question, and replied, "I don't know what happened to it, but the camera is unopened, and everything is there, you can check if you want."

"It's not about the camera, ma'am. The barcode isn't there. We can't resell it like this."

"Here's the camera that we bought from you guys—you take it back, and give me my money."

She avoided talking about the barcode, and didn't want to say anything about the rebate that she'd already received. I was trying to draw her attention to the fact, but didn't want to accuse her outright. I thought I could handle this on my own, and didn't want to call Cindy on her day off.

"I'm sorry, but we need the box to be in the same condition as when it was sold," I insisted.

Now the lady put a mean smile on her face, and said, "Listen, my husband is a lawyer. Please don't make me call him." She pulled out her cell phone and flipped it open, as a warning. Alexi and I looked at each other—trying to decide what to do. Although I had learned some things about lawsuits in America from talking to Cindy and observing people's behavior, this was the first time someone had come near to threatening to sue me. I was careful, and didn't take the lady's threat lightly, but at the same time I wasn't scared since I didn't think she could have sued me personally. I also wondered about what she could sue us for—we were just asking her to bring the box back in the same condition as when she bought it. She was trying to use her husband as a threat. I didn't change my stance.

"Perhaps you can ask your husband if he has the barcode."

"I can call him, but I am sure he doesn't know where it is." She already had the phone open, but instead of calling her husband, she flipped the phone closed. She stood there, looking at me, and Alexi. We didn't say anything and looked at her blankly, waiting for her to talk to her husband.

"Come on, guys, give me my money back, or I'm calling my husband, he's a lawyer."

I smiled at her, and said, "It would be nice if you asked him if he knows anything about the barcode. He may have cut it off and put it somewhere."

The lady opened her phone, scrolled through the contact list, hit the call button, and attached the phone to her ear. "I'll let you talk to him, but let me warn you ... he can be nasty." I had been working at ElectronicsHut a while at this point and had gotten used to rude customers of various kinds. Some called me an Arab, some accused me of lying, some said I couldn't speak English, and some said I was just incompetent. Most of the unruly people took their frustration out on me, but no one tried to harm or threaten me in any way. This lady was the first person I had encountered who had threatened me directly.

Every time she said, "My husband is a lawyer, don't make him come here," I wondered if the husband and wife were equally implicated in this fraud. I took a deep breath, and kept quiet. I looked at my watch—ten minutes were left before the store was supposed to close.

I could have told her to leave and come back the next day since we weren't supposed to stay inside the building after the mall closed. Then she would have been someone else's problem. I wouldn't have to deal with her. While these thoughts occurred to me, she said, "Honey, this guy isn't taking the camera back, can you talk to him?" She handed me the phone, straining her neck muscles as if to say, *Oops!*

Before I said anything, I heard the guy screaming on the other end, "I don't wanna hear anything, just put my fucking four hundred bucks back on the card, that's all." He hung up. I took the phone away from my ear, and looked at the lady.

She said, "I warned you, he can be rude."

I wanted to log out and tell the lady, *Ma'am, I am sorry, but my shift is over—it is 5:30, and I have plans for the evening. You can call your husband and tell him to come down here and sue the company. Good luck!* There was a risk that I might lose my job for saying all that and walking out on the customer, but Cindy had gotten to know me well enough to understand the situation, and forgive me. I didn't want to disappoint Cindy, but I also didn't want to return the money. I called her and explained the situation.

She said, "Don't worry, Deepak. Just deduct the mail-in-rebate money, return the rest of it, and send her on her way. If she gives you any trouble after that, call security."

I had put Cindy on the speakerphone so that she could be heard by all of us. I knew my interpretation of her message wouldn't have been as effective. Her commanding tone, no-non-sense language, and powerful voice turned the woman, who had been acting as if she were a rock star, into a chicken. She didn't say a word, and I didn't have to explain anything. I asked for her card and returned the money, minus the hundred dollars that she had already gotten back in the mail.

As the customer walked out, I took a deep breath and thought what an eventful two hours we'd had. The lady was definitely a drama queen—she had put up quite a show of threatening us and had almost forced us to return her the money. I wondered if her husband was really a lawyer. I would have thought that most people who go to law schools to be trained to win cases in courts and make big money wouldn't have spouses who go around lying for petty cash. Today was one of those rare days when I didn't have to take the abuse from a rude customer. I looked at the final numbers. The store had taken a hit with that big return. I usually felt deflated after a slow day of sales, but today was different. I closed the store and walked out of the mall whistling a happy tune.

CHAPTER TWENTY-FIVE

Post-Christmas Blues

Just before Christmas, people swarmed the store no matter what time of the day it was and bought anything that was available. We were having a difficult time keeping merchandise stocked. The new shipment that arrived every week didn't seem to be enough. We sold stuff straight out of the newly arrived cardboard boxes—we didn't have time to shelve the products after the UPS guy unloaded his truck. If we ran out of a particular item, people would ask the exact date of the next shipment.

Customers would make sure they were there before we got the boxes full of new goods. People who would ordinarily never want a demo product didn't hesitate to buy a dusty-looking kitchen CD player that had been on display since last Christmas. It seemed like everyone was happily giving their money to us—checks, credit cards, cash, whatever they had. I swiped hundreds of plastic cards, stamped thousands of dollars' worth of checks, and counted several hundred green American bills during the holiday season.

Watching Americans go crazy over shopping, I wondered what would happen if they didn't like the things they had bought from us during the last month. What if they came back and returned it all? What if they wanted their money back? It was scary to think about, and I didn't remember Cindy telling us about this. She had only talked about the brighter side of the golden quarter. If people did return the merchandise with the same intensity they'd bought it, the store would take a big hit, and so would the employees. I was worried about it, but didn't let the thought dampen my spirits, and I continued selling until the last day of the holiday season.

The store was closed on Christmas, and Cindy was kind enough to give me a couple of days off after that. I enjoyed the festival with my in-laws, ate good food, and put on a few pounds by the time we got back to Charlottesville. It was the 28th of December when I returned to work. I was scheduled to start at eleven in the morning. Cindy was supposed to open the store. I took the number 7 to work.

The bus driver looked extra bloated since I'd last seen him. He was sluggish in his movements and in the way he said "Haya-doin'?" I noticed there was a sense of misery about him. I had been riding the bus for quite a few months, and had gotten to know most of the drivers.

I asked him, "Is everything okay?"

He turned his head towards me, and said, "Ah, y'know how you feel after Christmas—fat and broke."

"Oh, okay," I said, dropped the quarters in the slot, and perched myself on the first available seat.

Usually, the passengers on the bus passed around a smile or two, but they acted different this day—serious, not so friendly. The bus arrived at its destination, and I said to the bus driver, "I hope you have a good day."

I heard him say, "I'll try" as I got off.

The mall was not playing its festive music anymore. The Christmas trees and wreaths were still there, but had been moved to the sides or backs of the stores. The place where kids had sat on Santa's lap and had their pictures taken looked like nothing had ever happened there. The shoppers weren't present in the same numbers. There were no children giggling, playing, running around, and screaming. The absence of noise, excitement, and buzz was palpable. All the kiosks that had sprung up around the holiday season were gone. Justin didn't have a long line in front of his store, and as I walked further, I saw Ben with a plate of pretzel samples walking around.

I went into my store, and saw Cindy talking with a customer in a flustered tone. She had a huge plastic bag sitting next to her, stuffed with something. I saw the customer giving his credit card to her, and then taking it back after she swiped. He stuffed the card into his wallet and walked out. She looked at me, and said, "You don't wanna look at our sales today."

"Why?"

"It's been an awful morning," she said.

I punched in my ID and pulled up the sales screen. At first, I wondered if Cindy was joking about having a bad morning since the total was nineteen hundred dollars. It had only been an hour since the store opened. I looked at Cindy, and she was still upset. I turned back to the screen, and noticed that it was actually negative nineteen hundred dollars—which meant we had to sell the same amount to get back to zero. I had witnessed days when we had taken big returns, but never had we taken back merchandise worth almost two thousand dollars this early in the morning. The day had just begun.

While I was still trying to take it in, and staring at the screen, I noticed something that made me dizzy. Out of the nineteen hundred, fourteen hundred was in my name. I took my eyes off the screen after a minute, and turned around to see if Cindy had anything to say. She had already returned to her chair. I stood there wondering if I would be able to recover from the day's negative total. I took three more returns in the next hour, and didn't make a single sale. The people who had spent hundreds of dollars without any hesitation until a few days ago had now gone into hiding.

The people who were in the mall had a different air about them—their mood had changed, the spirit was gone. It was strange to think that a festival in America can bring about such a drastic change in its citizens' behavior. After a month of fervor, joy, celebration, and extreme spending, people were showing withdrawal symptoms. The smiles had disappeared from their faces, the liveliness wasn't the same, and their body language was different. As shocked as I was to see the negative total on the computer screen, it pained me to watch the same people, who had been animated and bubbly a few days ago, with long faces. The departure of the festival that had brought so much happiness to everyone's lives seemed to have left them in a state of gloom.

I went to Cindy to ask her if it was normal to have so many returns in a single day. She said, "We do get a lot of returns after Christmas, but we just have to put up with it."

"How long does it go on for?"

"It'll get better come January." She smiled as if to say, *Don't worry.*

Working with Cindy for several months I had come to trust her, and to believe what she said. I relied on her as a leader and a competent manager. I had learned that whatever decisions she made would be for the good of her workers. She often preempted problems and solved them before they occurred, and if we got into trouble, she was always there to help us out. I took a deep breath when she said the returns were expected—and that they weren't supposed to last very long.

Now that the store was not doing much business, Cindy tried to space out employees' shifts when she scheduled us for work. I was supposed to work with Tom for the next three days. He had been around for the past week or so, but we were busy selling all the time and didn't get to know each other.

Since Tom had been a store manager in the past, he seemed to know a lot of things that only managers know—things that sales associates were not supposed to know. He knew how to get into the data system and change the price of a product, make it free, or delete certain things from the inventory of the store as if they had never existed. Sales associates were not trained to do these kinds of things, and if there was a need they were supposed to get the manager's approval. Tom often used his knowledge to facilitate his sales. When I first saw him do that, I thought I had missed something in training and I should know it. When I saw something funky happen on the computer screen, I'd ask him if he could show me how he did that. He would avoid my question, and change the topic.

I had been paying close attention to the different selling styles of my colleagues. They were each unique in their ways of approaching a customer, pitching a product, and closing a deal. I had learned the basic principles of marketing and sales in college in India, but working in an American retail electronics store had taught me the practical aspect of sales. Living in a college town where people from all over the world come to study and teach, I dealt with people from different countries, cultures, and backgrounds.

Since Charlottesville is surrounded by rural areas, the consumer base at our store was a checkerboard: people wearing traditional garb from Afghanistan, turban-clad Sikhs from India, college students sporting J-Crew wrinkled shorts and T-shirts, African Americans who spoke with a southern drawl, and Caucasians of different shades of white and pink, some wearing cowboy boots covered in dirt and hay. With such a variety of customers on the sales floor, there was no particular approach that would always work. Everyone had different needs, and a different style of shopping. I had learned to adapt myself to different kinds of shoppers, and approached them accordingly. I knew not to waste my time trying to sell a radio scanner to a Chinese student who spoke very little English, explaining the features of an iPod to a lady who looked to be in her nineties, or showing a portable cassette player to a nineteen-year-old college student who thought he was too cool for something like that.

Generally, foreigners came to buy plug adapters so that they could use their foreign-bought gizmos in America. Grandparents came to buy home phones with big buttons and loud ringers, and young college students were mostly interested in the latest cell phones that would allow them to watch TV or play video games. Each group had a sales language that it preferred to hear. Older people liked it when I made things simple to understand, opened the box, demonstrated the product, and spent extra time with them. They would say, "Thanks so much for showing us how it works, because the last time I bought a phone, I just couldn't get it to make a call." Foreigners liked coming to me because of my brown skin and accent. Apparently I looked like someone who would know all the halal-meat shops in town, or someone who would speak perfect Spanish. People from rural parts of Virginia seemed to understand me better when I inserted an extra syllable in each word I spoke.

I thought different customers should be treated differently, but Tom didn't think so. He defied all the commonly accepted sales techniques, etiquettes, and procedures. He had a completely different style of selling that I hadn't seen before. He seemed to have only one goal in mind: sell a cell phone to anyone and everyone. And he did.

If he saw someone lurking around the cell phone wall while he was selling something to another customer, he would leave in the middle of the procedure to approach the other person. He would ask me, "Deepak, could you finish this sale, I'll be right back." I would apologize to the customer for the abrupt break while she looked at Tom in amazement.

If he saw a six-year-old playing in the store, he would ask him, "You want a free cell phone, buddy?" The kid would look at him with a sparkle in his eyes. "Go get your momma, tell her I have a free phone for you." The kid would run off to get his mother. The next minute a woman would come in and say, "Hey, did someone tell my kid he can get a free phone today?"

Tom would reply, "Yes, I did. You want one?" About twenty minutes later, the woman would walk out with a bag full of cell phone accessories, and a cell phone in her hand.

I thought I had learned a few things about selling, but most times I would just stand there and watch him sell with my mouth wide open. The people who came to return a Christmas gift never left without getting something else if Tom was helping them. He wouldn't shut his mouth until they gave up and bought whatever he suggested. I thought it was great for the store that he was there; otherwise we would never get out of the hole, and would finish most days with negative totals.

But another part of my mind thought that he was pressuring the customers too much. Sometimes he seemed to push every limit to get a sale. Most of the customers didn't leave feeling entirely happy after dealing with him. It felt as if they couldn't say no to anything Tom offered; he had an answer to every excuse the customers came up with for not buying something, and he always seemed to win. He often used a metaphor to describe his selling technique: *You try to run over every squirrel you see on the road, and you will get six out of ten.* His customers sometimes reminded me of squirrels scampering away to save their lives.

After about two weeks, Cindy called a meeting. She reviewed everyone's sales. We all did well, but Tom's sales were way more than anyone else's. Cindy often praised us if we did well, but she didn't say anything when she looked at Tom's numbers. Later in the day when Tom was on his lunch break, she brought Ron, Jackie, and me together and said, "There's something not right with Tom's sales. According to his sales figures, he's made more money than most managers in the company. It can't be right."

No one had anything to say. He was pushing customers more than they liked, but there weren't any clearly defined rules against it. In fact, most managers liked their associates to be more assertive with the customers. While we stood there, Tom returned from lunch with a large fountain-soda cup in one hand and a sheet of paper in the other.

He came up to us, and set down what looked like the spreadsheet of his sales total. He grinned widely and let out a loud burp. "If I can sell like this every month I'll be making the same amount of money as I did when I was a manager," he said and smiled. We gave him a blank look. "Isn't it cool to be making as much as a manager and not have any responsibilities?" he asked—and looked at Cindy. "It isn't all that bad getting demoted, after all." Cindy didn't say anything, and walked back to her office.

Tom continued using this style of selling. On a daily basis, his sales equaled the total of three sales associates put together. He was doing everything to make a sale—convince, confuse, and corrupt. He was a good talker and had a lot of knowledge about products. If a customer was knowledgeable, he would answer every question she could come up with. If he realized a customer didn't know enough and was unsure about buying, he would try to confuse her by mentioning the technical nitty-gritty of the product. When someone was too smart and said no to everything he offered, he would try to give away a free accessory with a product to make a sale. It often worked, since most people said yes to getting something for free that would cost them thirty dollars or more in normal circumstances.

One day, Tom and I were supposed to close together. It was a slow evening. I had sold only two hundred dollars' worth of merchandise. Tom was getting frustrated because no one was coming into the store. He said, "I can sell anything to anyone, but people need to come in." He hadn't sold much, and it looked like he was going to end up with a small total that day. Around eight, an hour before we were supposed to close, a middle-aged black man walked in with a cell phone in his hand. As soon as he stepped in, Tom, who had been sitting on the counter, jumped off, and raced towards him.

"How is it going?" he said.

"Doin' awright. How about you?" said the man, who was wearing overalls covered in red dirt. His face was dusty, and his hands were rough—soot was visible in the folds of his fingers.

His big yellow boots left a mark on the carpet of the store. He appeared to be a construction worker.

"Good, what can I help you with?" Tom asked.

"Need to pay my cell phone bill," said the customer. I watched Tom getting a little discouraged since the person already had a cell phone. I was curious to see how he would try to sell something to this guy.

"Alright, how much do you want to pay today?"

"Let me see," he said, and shoved his hand into the wide pocket of his overalls. He pulled out a bunch of crumpled bills and set them on the counter. As he separated the tens and fives, Tom asked him, "How do you feel about getting a new cell phone today?"

"I am locked in a contract, can't do it for another two months."

"We can set you up with another company, you'll get a free cell phone. Don't even need to pay your bill."

"Really?" The construction worker looked up, and said, "What about my contract with the current company?"

"Don't worry about that. Can I have your ID for a second?" The customer gave him his driver's license. Tom did a quick credit check. He tapped his fingers on the counter while the website took its time to show the result.

"You know what? You can walk out of here without spending a single penny, and get a spanking new cell phone," said Tom with a big grin. The guy looked at him with no expression. Before he could say anything, Tom said, "Come here, let's pick your phone." Tom walked to the cell phone wall. The customer followed. "These two are free, and this one is thirty bucks ... I guess you would wanna go for a free cell phone, right?" I said. The customer shrugged his shoulders, and didn't say anything.

"Alright, I'll be right back." Tom walked to the backroom and, within no time, he was back with a new cell phone. Tom was hurrying and not giving the man any chance to decide against buying the cell phone. Frenetically, he opened the box, ripped open the pouch that contained the phone with his teeth, spat out the tiny piece of plastic, scanned the barcodes from the back of the phone, and within a few minutes he set the guy up with a new cell phone monthly plan.

Before the customer got a change to say anything, Tom printed out the two-year contract papers, gave him a pen, and pointed his finger at a blank saying, "Now you can go and buy yourself a bottle of beer, and talk on your phone as much you want. You don't have to pay any bill until next month." The tired man looked at him and smiled. Tom rubbed his index finger on the blank line suggesting that he sign there. He signed, and before he could ask any questions, Tom gave him his new cell phone. He said, "It's workin' already." The phone in the hands of the customer started ringing. Tom gave him his receipt and said, "Have a good night."

The customer stood there and looked at the cell phone, the receipt, and the plastic bag in his hands. He didn't move for a few seconds, and then said, "Listen, you didn't tell me what would happen to the contract with my current cell phone company."

It seemed as if Tom were trying to avoid this question. "Just use this phone, and don't worry about it," he said.

"What do you mean 'Don't worry about it?'"

"I mean, don't pay that bill, and they'll automatically cut it off."

"Won't they charge me some two hundred bucks for getting out of the contract before time?"

"They won't," said Tom, not making eye contact with him.

The construction worker looked at him, and then looked at me, and said, "Is he telling the truth?"

I had been watching Tom deal with this customer the entire time. Although I was standing at a distance, I knew that the customer knew that I was a witness to the whole thing. By asking me if Tom was telling the truth he put me in an awkward position. I didn't know what to say, since I knew Tom was lying. I couldn't just say he was lying because it would have caused a confrontation. Also, if I did try to correct Tom, I suspected, the customer might wonder why I hadn't told him earlier.

The problem was that Tom knew more about rules, contracts, and cell phones in general than I did, and even when I knew that there was something off in his dealings with the customers, I didn't have the confidence to intervene. I thought that he must know something I didn't.

The customer's questioning eyes continued to stare at me for an answer. Tom looked at me as if he wanted to say, *Come on, Deepak, say yes.* As a colleague of Tom's, one part of me said I should side with him and tell the person he was telling the truth, but I also thought about something called "blowing the whistle" that I had learned in training.

Since the customer was still waiting for an answer, I said, "Probably, but I am not sure—he knows more than I do." I stepped away with a safe answer. Tom had made the sale, and it was time to close the store soon. I thought about what I had done, and what I should have done. I felt as if I hadn't told the truth to the customer. I had taken Tom's side by being silent. I didn't feel very proud of myself.

I went home and continued thinking about what had happened. I wanted to tell Cindy about the whole thing, but I had the next day off. I didn't think it was a good idea to wait until I got back to work. I called her soon after the store opened the next day.

"Cindy, do you have a minute?"

"Yes, what do you need?" She sounded as if she were busy. I said, "I wanted to tell you about something that happened last night at the store."

"What's that?"

"Tom sold a phone to this guy and—"

"Hold on a second, this is really important, Deepak. I'm gonna have to call you back, I am with a customer right now."

"Okay," I said.

She called back a minute later. "Awright, tell me what happened."

I told her the whole story. She listened carefully, and said, "Thank you so much for telling me this, and I'll see you tomorrow."

I felt that even though I hadn't told the customer that Tom was not telling the truth, I needed to make Cindy aware of it. The next day I showed up at work. As usual, I hung up my coat, put my food in the fridge, and looked at the schedule pasted on the bathroom door to see who else was coming in today. I noticed a thick black line running across the sheet. I looked closely to see what had been crossed off. It was Tom's schedule.

I turned and saw Cindy standing behind me. I looked at her and she said, "I informed the district manager about what you told me, and she faxed me a letter asking me to terminate Tom immediately." I didn't know what to say. Although I had no idea that my report could lead to Tom's dismissal, I had the feeling that Cindy had been waiting for a reason to fire him. While I stood there looking blankly at the floor, she picked up her purse from her chair, took out a pack of Marlboro Lights, and said, "Awright, I am gonna go smoke a cigarette."

Just before she walked out the door, she turned back and said, "By the way I called the customer. He came in and returned the phone that Tom sold him. You did a good job by reporting the matter to me." She gave me two thumbs up and shut the door behind her.

CHAPTER TWENTY-SIX

A Handful of Dimes

When I first got hired, my number one goal was to not get fired. The job seemed daunting, and I was worried that I could lose it if I didn't do more than what was required from a regular employee. I focused hard on learning about products, their names and their uses. I paid a lot of attention to what customers were asking for, and how they were describing what they wanted.

After almost a year of selling electronics, I had learned more than what was required to keep my job. I was aware of most of the things the job had taught me, but there were a few things I didn't even realized I had learned. I had stopped assuming that a dad who brought his ten-year-old son to get him an iPod would automatically pay for it. Half the time he made his little boy spend his pocket money. I had learned not to assume that two women who came in wearing matching pink miniskirts, tank tops, sparkly lipstick, high heels, and glittery purses, were sisters or friends. Half of the time they turned out to be mother and daughter. I had learned not to be surprised, or disturbed, when a young mother told her toddler son in public, "Come on, let's go, Duane. When Daddy gets outta jail, he's gonna get you that Robocop for Christmas," or when a middle-aged man said to me in front of his ten-year-old daughter, "I need a camera phone so I can send my naked pictures to all my bitches."

Most times I was able to tell what customers wanted before they finished their questions. I was able to decode the southern drawl, and had toned down my Indian accent—people on the other end of a phone conversation no longer asked to speak to someone who spoke English. I also had acquired local knowledge without even trying: I knew the zip codes of many counties and small towns around Charlottesville.

It came to me as a surprise when Cindy told me that I had become the top salesperson in the store. She also said that my sales figures were the best among other branches of the company in the city, and occasionally, I managed to get into the bracket of the top five salespeople in the district—which included hundreds of stores. Cindy started setting me up as an example in her meetings: "He used to walk away from the customers, and look at him now," she would tell the new employees to motivate them. Cindy told them that I made good money, and that I was one of the best-paid employees in the entire district. I was making more money than most new employees, but the difference wasn't huge. I didn't know what to think of all this since my lifestyle hadn't changed much since I had first started. I still thought hard before buying a second cup of coffee. I still used public transport, and brought home-cooked food to work.

One day when I was putting up the merchandise, I noticed Ron coming in with his lunch bag hanging from his shoulder, looking down at the floor, walking slowly. He usually moved with a tired gait, but this was different. Just to check how his mood was, I said hello. He didn't respond and walked past me, continuing to look down. I waited for him to come back onto the sales floor. He appeared after a few minutes. He laid his hands on the counter, bent his head down, and let out a big sigh. I went to him, put my hand on his shoulder, and said, "Are you okay, Ron?"

"I'll be okay one of these days."

"What's the matter?"

"I have to," he sighed again, "go file my bankruptcy papers today. Can't afford to make payments on my mortgage anymore." I looked at him. His eyes were moist. "I don't make enough money here. Gotta find something else," he said. There was nothing I could say to make him feel better. All I could do was to lay my hand on his shoulder for a minute and squeeze it. I walked back, feeling helpless, and picked the other items from the box to shelve them.

After a few minutes, Ron came to me, bent down, letting out a slight groan, picked up a cassette player and placed it on the shelf. He came back and picked another product out of the box and shelved it.

I said, "Ron, it's okay, I can do it. You can relax for a while."

He bent down, holding his knee with one hand, picked up something else, and said, "It's awright. I gotta do what I gotta do."

I felt bad for Ron. His age and health problems often brought to mind several friends and colleagues of my dad. Mr. Dube was one of them. He was potbellied, almost completely bald, and had arthritis, high blood pressure, and diabetes. He worked for a government-owned power company, and could barely manage to make himself sit on his twenty-year-old cream-colored Bajaj scooter to get to the office. There he sat on a wooden chair that had a tatty cushion on it and moaned all day about how his life sucked in every possible way. I felt bad for Mr. Dubeq, too, but at least he had a government job that was stable and came with a pension when he retired. He had two obedient sons who were studying to be engineers. Ron was almost fifty, financially insecure, with the medical problems of a sixty-year-old, and had no one to help.

Ron was not the only person who was having a hard time keeping up with expenses. Jackie was always under pressure to sell more and make more commissions so that she could pay for her child's babysitter, get her car fixed, and pay the rent. It hadn't dawned on me that people were not able to support themselves with the money they were making. Since I didn't have to pay any child support, make payments on a mortgage, or a car loan, I hadn't realized that supporting a family with this retail job could be so difficult. I wasn't paying any attention to my checks because I had a direct deposit arrangement. The money went into my bank account every two weeks. Most of the time, I didn't have to deal with the finances because my wife paid most of the bills.

When I heard Cindy telling everyone that I made good money, I became curious. I wondered how good "good" money was, since everyone else at work was struggling to pay their bills. I logged onto the company website to take a look at my last paycheck. Since it was my first job in the United States, I didn't know what amount was considered to be a good salary, and had nothing to compare it with. I looked at my recent paychecks, and I saw that I was averaging around nine hundred dollars a month. To keep it in perspective, and to be able to compare, I converted that to Indian rupees. I was shocked to discover that it was only 30 percent more than I had been making at my last job in India. I had not thought about it this way before.

It made me remember how, before I came to the United States, Holly had tried to convince me to keep my job in India while she visited me on breaks until she finished her work at UVA. Her hesitation didn't dissuade me from taking the leap to come to the United States. In fact, I had started wondering why she wanted me to stay back in India.

Now, making only 30 percent more money, I was somehow living in America, where the cost of living was at least four times more expensive than it was in India. Just our rent for the apartment in Charlottesville took most of my salary. I realized I would not be able to meet the expenses had my wife not also been earning. It made sense why my colleagues were having such a difficult time supporting their families on such a paltry amount.

I went home, thought about it, and discussed the situation with Holly. She said she hadn't wanted to complain about my small paychecks because I had a tough time finding a job in the first place, and when I found one, I struggled to get adjusted. She said she hadn't wanted to stress me out by bringing it up. When I told her about my colleagues struggling, she wasn't surprised. She talked about how difficult it is to get a better-paying job if you don't have a college degree. I realized this described what was happening with Ron and Jackie. They were barely managing to pay the rent or mortgage for their homes; I couldn't imagine them being able to provide higher education for their children. It seemed that they were caught in a vicious cycle.

When Cindy told me that I was doing a good job as a sales associate, she also mentioned that I was due for a vacation. She came to me and said, "Deepak, I just wanted you to know that you will be entitled to a two-week *paid* vacation in a few days." She gave me a big grin. I thanked her, but wondered about what the hourly rate was going to be, since my income was mostly based on commissions. Before I asked, she said, "You will get minimum wage for two weeks."

I didn't feel very enthusiastic about taking the vacation because I could make more than six dollars an hour if I chose not go and worked instead. My wife suggested we should take the opportunity and go to India. It had been quite a while since I had first come to the United States, so I agreed with her and planned to visit my parents.

CHAPTER TWENTY-SEVEN

India Visit

After being in the United States for almost two years—six months of waiting for my work permit, three months of job searching, and a year now at ElectronicsHut—it was time to visit India. I told Cindy I wanted to go for six weeks. She didn't think I could go for that long, but she told me she would work something out. She wanted me to visit home, but she also didn't want to lose me as an employee. After a couple of days she told me I could take part of the trip as paid time off and the rest as a leave of absence. I agreed.

I had never been away from my parents for this long. It seemed like a decade to me. I had been in touch with them over phone calls and letters. They didn't have a computer at home, so no video chats. I was anxious about seeing my family. Would my mother have accumulated more wrinkles? Would my father have more grey hairs? Would my sister's son have grown taller? I was also looking forward to seeing my friends. I didn't know what to expect, and I didn't know what was expected of me.

Over those first two years in the United States, I had been very careful about telling my family and friends about my job in America. There was no way I could have told my mother that I worked as a salesman in a retail store. She would have been mortified. When I first got the job, I had told them that I was working in sales in an electronics company, but I always avoided answering questions about the details of my work. I was careful not to say that I was going to open the store or close the store, or that I was shelving items. My mother was the one who was most inquisitive, but she gave me the benefit of doubt. She believed what I told her, because I was in a different country, a different culture. Although she had never traveled abroad, she was attuned to the world through newspapers and television. Often times, she called me to let me know of a possible hurricane or snowstorm that was headed in my direction. I got the idea that she knew that I was not entirely happy with my job. She would often tell me to continue looking for other positions.

I had to sit down and talk with Holly about going to India and spending nearly two months with my family. It wasn't just me who would have to be careful about mentioning anything about my job, but also Holly. She didn't understand what the big deal was, and why I couldn't just say that I worked in retail. I had to explain to her the gravity of the situation. I reminded her how hard it had been for her to tell her family that she had decided to marry an Indian. I hadn't understood, when I was still in India, why she couldn't call her parents from Lucknow to tell them about me. I had no idea how her family in Pennsylvania—who grew up and spent their entire lives within a twenty-mile radius—would react to her daughter marrying someone from a different country, a different culture, a different race. They didn't understand why she had to marry a Deepak, and not a Duane or a Danny, someone who had gone to high school with her, or at least lived within the same zip code. There was more to the story than I understood at the time. Likewise, it took Holly a while to realize that for my family, quitting a plush job in India and working a retail job in the United States was not just a bad career move, but also a matter of taboo. That she needed to talk as little as possible about my job was very important.

We arrived at the train station in Lucknow on a blazing June afternoon. The smell of the heat, human sweat, fried bread, mango peels, and sunbaked urine brought back India in one instant. The staccato voice of the lady announcing the trains on the speaker sounded like a lullaby to me.

My parents had come to pick me up. My mother saw me stepping out of the train and started crying. My father stood a few feet away, acting tough. I noticed he was looking at me from the corner of his eyes. Maybe he was noticing my clothes, my shoes. I wanted to look like the same guy who had spent thirty years with them under the same roof. A few days before I had left Charlottesville, I had been thinking of wearing the same shirt to India that I had worn when I'd left Lucknow two years ago. I ended up wearing an Old Navy shirt, dark-green corduroy pants, and a pair of New Balance sneakers. My mother couldn't take her eyes off my face, a face that was much rounder than before. I knew I had put on weight in America. I had come to like donuts and cookies. I bent down to touch their feet.

When we got home, the aroma of freshly made *roti*s overwhelmed me. Tears welled up in my eyes. Those finely rolled, round pieces of bread puffing up on the flames of my mother's stove were what I had missed most. I hadn't come even close to anything like that in America. Every brick of the house seemed to smell of it. Maybe my nose had become sensitive by living in a too-sterile environment in the United States, or maybe I had been so deprived of the smell of the warm *roti* that it hit me strongly. It was the smell of home, the fragrance of my mother's love. I walked around the house and opened the family armoire. I noticed my light-blue shirt and green pants, washed and neatly ironed. It seemed as if I had never left. I found myself in a sea of emotions.

Soon my mother started bringing out the food that she had been preparing for the last two days to welcome Holly and me. Everyone gathered around us. We ate and talked until two in the morning.

We woke up late the next day. I heard Neera, a short-statured lady who had been a maid in our house for many years. She washed dishes and swept and mopped the floor twice a day, seven days a week. She gave me a big smile. I was happy to see her. Neera wanted to hear our stories from America. What kind of food did we eat, what kind of car did we drive, and what kind of home did we have? I showed her pictures and videos of our life on the laptop, and tried to explain how things worked in our home.

Neera asked me if I had a maid in America. I told her most people in America cleaned their houses and washed the dishes themselves. Only rich people could afford maids. Astonished, she asked me how we managed without one. She couldn't close her mouth when I said I was the one who washed the dishes. My mother looked at me with a frown. When Neera left, she said to me, "Now that you have told Neera you wash dishes in your home in America, she will tell the entire city. What will people say? Do you have any idea?"

I had forgotten that I used to be careful before I said anything in front of my mother. I had gotten used to living without her looking over my shoulder all the time. Washing dishes had struck me as demeaning in the beginning, but I got over that very quickly. I found it easier to get the dishes out of my way myself than to wait for someone else to do them. I remembered how much of a hassle it used to be in Lucknow when Neera didn't show up once in a while. Instead of doing the dishes with our own hands, we went looking for Neera, asking around other homes if she had come to work. We would waste a lot of time waiting for her.

My mother did a lot of other chores around the house, like laundry, cooking, and tidying, but she didn't want to get rid of Neera. It was a matter of status for her. She didn't want to be seen as someone who couldn't afford even a maid. I had never cared about status in general, and after living in America and working in retail, status was at the bottom of the pile of my worries. I looked at my mother's angered face and thought I couldn't wait to know what she would say if I told her about my job in the United States.

A few days later, I went to Hazratganj, my favorite shopping area in Lucknow. I wanted to see if my *chaiwallah*, tea vendor, Ramesh, was still there. When I had lived in Lucknow, there hadn't been a day when I didn't go to him for a cup of cardamom chai. He ran the chai shop with his wife, Kamla. She usually lurked in the background doing chores like washing teacups, grinding ginger, and tidying the shop, while Ramesh took care of the business. Sometimes she ran the shop when Ramesh did errands around town.

As I walked down the alley to his shop, he saw me coming from a distance. He raised his hand and said, "After a long time?"

"Yes, it's been a long time."

"Where were you?" There were some customers standing around his giant aluminum pot of chai. I didn't feel comfortable announcing that I had moved to the States.

I had never asked Ramesh how much money he made, but if I were to guess, I'd say it wasn't more than a one hundred dollars a month. He and his wife fired up the stove right at dawn and shut the shop only when it was time to sleep at night. One of the reasons why I went to him was because I was sure to get a cup of chai no matter what time of day it was. I wasn't his friend, but I was a regular at his place. He had gotten to know me over the period of a few years.

When he asked me where I had been, at first I didn't feel comfortable announcing that I had moved to the United States. It wasn't unlike driving a Mercedes to see your friend, a friend who was struggling to make ends meet. Moving to America wasn't like moving to Bangladesh. Moving to America, to a lot of people in India, meant upward mobility, prosperity, and money. I could only imagine what it would mean to a streetside tea vendor.

I walked up to him and asked how he had been. He told me he was fine and that he was working harder than before, because he was saving to marry off his daughter. He gave me a steaming cup of chai with a spoonful of *malai* on top. The extra cream was his way of welcoming me. He asked me again, "Where did you go?"

"I was in America," I said, and looked at him. He didn't say anything. A few minutes later, he said, "Amrika?"

"Yes, Amrika."

"You never told me."

"Yes, I didn't get to meet a lot of people before I left."

"I am a small man. No one has time to meet people like me."

"No, no, Ramesh. I actually missed your chai a lot in America."

"*Achha*? There's no chai there?"

"Not like yours."

"Take us with you. My wife will make chai for you and I will make you good food."

I laughed.

"Really. Take us with you," Kamla said. "I will make good chai for you, with double *malai*." She was wearing a sari, covering her head with its end. Before I had moved to the States, I never thought of her as anyone but a lady who sold chai. Our interactions were limited. She handed me a cup of chai and I gave her the money. Not many words exchanged.

I looked at her in a different light after coming back from the United States. She reminded me of Julie at Starbucks in the mall. Kamla and Julie did pretty much the same thing, and I knew them both for the same reason—hot beverages. Julie was a student at the university. She worked part-time at the coffee shop to make some extra money. She didn't own the shop, but Kamla did. Julie didn't want to work more than fifteen hours a week, and Kamla *had* to work fifteen hours a day. Julie's chai cost more than two dollars a cup, and Kamla made a cup of chai for ten cents.

For Julie, working at Starbucks was a temporary thing. For Kamla, selling chai on streets was her life. Julie could work part-time for six months as a barista, and, since the job was just to give her some pocket money, she could easily save enough to buy a plane ticket to travel to India. Kamla could never sell enough cups of chai to travel to America. The more I thought of Julie and Kamla the more pensive I became.

Ramesh offered me his stool to sit down. He had never done that before. I ended up having three cups of chai. I sat there watching the couple for a while, and then I took out a twenty-rupee bill to pay, but Ramesh refused to take any money. Again, this was something he had never done before. I smiled. He smiled back. I had wanted to pay fifteen rupees, forty cents, for the three cups of chai and leave the rest as a tip. By giving five rupees more, I wanted to rid myself of the burden of living in America. Ramesh didn't want to accept twenty rupees, because he was holding out for something bigger. He folded my fingers over my money. I took his leave and promised to come back and see him.

"I'm a poor man," he said as I walked away. "Don't forget me, big man."

I spent a lot of my time in Lucknow visiting friends and family. While Holly was busy doing field research for her doctorate, I went to the mausoleums in the old city and sat on its expansive, wide steps—one of my favorite places to relax and reflect. As days passed, we started thinking about what we wanted to take back with us to the United States. There was a long list, but what I really wanted was to buy some recent Indian films. I went to town, looking for DVDs. I walked into an old music shop. The place also sold CD players, TVs, digital cameras, and things like that. The shop had been around for several decades in Lucknow. A young man behind the counter displayed several films before me. I picked out four. They cost ten dollars each. I noticed the salesman studying me, running his eyes top to bottom.

"Do you live somewhere outside?" By *outside* he meant abroad. His questioning made me realized that this was the first time I had bought a DVD in Lucknow. Living in India, I didn't own a DVD player. I always watched movies in theaters. The salesman probably didn't see very many locals who came to buy DVDs for Indian films.

I paused before I answered his question. I took a look at the DVDs. All of them had a price sticker. I said, "Yes," expecting a follow-up question.

"I can tell," he smiled, and said, "England, sir?"

"No, U.S.A."

"Ok, ok. Do you want more movies? We have a very large collection. Old movies also."

He had a pleasing manner about him. I told him to show more. He brought out a stack of DVDs. While I browsed through them, he mentioned that he had digital cameras in the store. The scene looked much too familiar to me. I imagined him as myself. I had been doing the same thing a few days ago, save for a few differences. I looked at him and smiled. The guy looked to be around twenty-five years of age. He was tall for an Indian, had a long face and a blade of a nose. I didn't know the guy and had never seen him when I lived in Lucknow. I wanted to see how he would react if I told him that I did the same kind of work as him. He didn't seem like a threat, someone who could tell my family about my job in the States.

"What's your name?"

"Vikas, sir."

"Vikas, can I tell you something?"

"Sure, sir."

"I do what you do."

"What, sir?"

"I have the same job as you in America."

"Okay, sir. But, sir, how much is your salary?"

I told him I made around fifteen hundred dollars a month, about seventy-five thousand rupees, but it fluctuated.

"Sir, see this is the difference. I do the same thing here and my salary is only six thousand rupees per month." He looked dreamy-eyed. "Can I get a job there, sir?"

"Vikas, fifteen hundred dollars is not much in America. I pay $750 in rent."

He started laughing from disbelief.

"The houses come studded with pearls and diamonds in America?"

"No, they don't."

"Why so expensive then?"

"I don't know. Everything is expensive there."

"Sir, I've heard that everyone has a car there? Do you maintain a car?" I knew by *maintaining a car* most Indians meant that you didn't just own car to show off, but you actually used it on a daily basis.

"Yes. It is actually my wife's car," I told him.

"You got it in dowry?"

"You can say so," I smiled.

"This is why America is the richest country, sir. In this job, I can never maintain a car."

"But you don't need a car."

"I don't need it, but I don't want to ride my bicycle all my life. It'd be embarrassing if I had to take my wife to a movie on the back of my bicycle." I laughed and asked him if he was married. "No, sir, not yet. My father is looking for a nice girl."

"Maybe you'll get a car in dowry," I said, jokingly.

"In this job? Never. No one will give a car in dowry to a man who makes only six thousand rupees. Also, petrol is fifty rupees a liter. Can't afford it." This made me think of Holly's Oldsmobile and the gas prices in America. I told Vikas that gas was

40 percent cheaper in America and Americans still thought it was too expensive.

"Sir, please, take me there," he laughed.

Vikas made only a little over a hundred dollars a month, but he didn't seem unhappy or bogged down by his life. He had a glint in his eyes. I realized we had been talking for quite a while. I bought eight DVDs instead of four. I thought that might make him happy. I took his leave and he said, "Come again, sir. I felt very good talking to you."

"Sure. I also enjoyed talking to you, Vikas."

As I walked away, I wondered if I was acting differently toward Vikas than I would have before leaving. Was I trying to be nice to him, because I now understood what it was like to be a salesman? Maybe, I thought.

Vikas and Ramesh were not the only people who wanted me to help them get to the United States. Some of my friends whom I had played cricket with on the streets of Lucknow asked me to find them American wives. They asked if Holly had a sister. They were only half joking about this. The five dollar shirt that I had bought on 75 percent clearance from Old Navy misled them into believing that I had become rich. I had gifted a few shirts to a few of my friends, except that I'd peeled off the orange clearance sticker and left the original price tag on. They introduced me to their friends as an NRI—nonresident Indian. Any Indian who lived in a different country was technically a nonresident Indian, but the acronym NRI was reserved for Indians who lived in the United States, the United Kingdom, Australia, or Europe. In other words, my friends wanted to say to their friends, "Meet my rich friend from America."

They sometimes looked up to me, and sometimes hated me for having made it to the United States. One of my friends, Saket, would often smoke a cigarette, puff up the smoke, and then give me a naughty smile without saying anything. I knew what that smile meant. It meant, *You lucky bastard.*

I would be lying if I said I didn't enjoy his envy, but a part of me wanted to tell him the truth—the hardship, the emotional distress, the humiliation I had gone through. I was afraid he might laugh at me for quitting my job in India to move to the States. He was doing quite well for himself in Lucknow. He drove a Hyundai sedan, had an expensive phone, and owned a mansion of a house, but he still thought I was better off than him. The idea of America was novel to him. When I told him I sometimes felt like moving back to India, he said, "Are you crazy? Do you know that every day a thousand people line up at two in the morning in the hope of getting an American visa at the U.S. embassy in New Delhi?"

Living with my parents, after spending almost two years without them, was quite different. My parents thought of me as the same person who had always lived with them. They hadn't changed, but I had. I had gone from missing them a lot in the United States to getting used to not having them around. All of a sudden I was with them again. My mother's constant nagging had never seemed more annoying to me. The lack of privacy also took some getting used to. I had never lived with my parents as a married man. Holly and I never really displayed affection for each other in public, but we had to be extra careful around my parents. My mother and father and all the relatives who came to visit us didn't think it was important to knock before they entered our bedroom.

Still, there was constant pressure from everyone about when we were going to make them grandparents, aunts, and uncles, and so on. Everyone asked, "When are you going to give us the good news?" I had come up with an American way of answering their question, which made them recoil from embarrassment. "We are trying," I said, which to my friends and family sounded like a far too-explicit statement about what was happening in that bedroom, even though they never actually saw.

The remaining time in India went fast, and then we were on the plane again—back to Charlottesville. I had to be at work the next day. I was excited about bringing my colleagues the gifts I'd picked out. I took the bus, and arrived at work on time. I saw Cindy at the counter by herself.

She smiled and said, "Welcome back!" I thanked her and laid the plastic bag that said *Lucknow Chikan Palace* on the counter. She said, "What's that, Deepak?"

"I brought something from Lucknow for you guys."

"Aww," she said, and craned her neck to take a look. I had given her a pink *kurti*, a hand-embroidered top. She took it and held it in front of her face, trying to see how it looked. I asked her if Ron and Jackie were on the schedule that day. I saw her expression turn immediately from happy to sad. She paused for a second, and said, "This is a really nice dress, Deepak, thank you so much for bringing it." I didn't know why she had changed the subject, so I asked again.

"Umm, this is what happened while you were gone."

"What?"

"They both quit." I couldn't believe what she had said.

"What, why?"

"Jackie was having some personal problems. Something to do with her boyfriend, I don't know. She said she wanted to spend more time with her kid, and think about what she wanted to do."

"And Ron?" I asked.

"Yeah, he said he found another job ... I don't know what the story is, but that's what he told me." I put their gifts back into the plastic bag. Cindy looked at me, and said, "I know, Deepak. I miss them too." I didn't say anything. I wasn't prepared for this news. I had learned a lot from them, and they had become quite good friends, almost family. I knew they were going through financial crises, and that's what must have caused them to quit their jobs. Cindy told me she had had to hire some more people to replace them.

The next day I took the bus to work, remembering the time I had spent with Ron and Jackie. I thought about how Jackie had helped me with my first sale, and how she always saved me when I had to deal with a difficult customer, how much patience she showed when I asked her questions while she was in the middle of a sale herself, and how she had taught me to be a good sales-person. I reflected on my time with Ron—how he hadn't liked me in the beginning, but had helped me anyway, and told me I needed to learn to speak English. The two people who had taught me about electronics and sales, and had helped me to keep my job, had ended up losing their own jobs. I felt very sad. I didn't feel like going to work. I wasn't sure if I wanted to work there anymore.

I arrived at the store, hoping Ron and Jackie would magically appear from somewhere. Cindy was sitting in her usual place doing something on her computer. She turned to me and said, "Deepak, I wanted to talk to you about something."

I looked at her inquisitively and said, "Okay."

"You have come a long way since you first started. I am impressed with what you have achieved as a sales associate. A lot of employees have come and gone since you have been here, and you have learned a lot from them and you've trained a lot of them. You are a role model for most new employees, and I would like you to consider becoming a manager—you are an asset to the company."

I wasn't sure how to feel. I was sad that Ron and Jackie weren't there, but it felt good to hear Cindy praise me and encourage me. I said, "Thanks a lot, Cindy, but can I think about it?"

"Of course, you can take your time," she said, and smiled. "I also wanted to tell you that I hired a new guy. His name is Tony. He is on lunch right now."

"Okay," I said, and walked onto the sales floor.

There were no customers. I stood in the middle of the store and looked around. I took a walk and gazed at the cell phone wall, the media wall, the watch battery section, at the fluorescent ceiling lights, at the floor, and at the counter. Reflecting on what Cindy had just told me, I realized that about a year ago I had struggled to sell a watch battery, labored to program a radio scanner, hid from the customers because I couldn't understand what they wanted, and got a month's notice to perform or leave. This sales floor was the place where I strove to make my first sale, and suffered—being ridiculed, laughed at, and made to feel incompetent—as a foreign sales associate.

I found it hard to believe that Cindy, who wasn't thrilled to have me on the sales team, and who had once told me I had a month to prove myself or she would fire me, had just said that I was a role model, and that I was an asset to the company. While I stood there and remembered various incidents that had taken place during my time at the store, a tall, young man wearing a blue button-down shirt and khaki pants walked in. I realized I hadn't logged in yet, but before I could do that I saw him standing before me, looking at me strangely, as if he were trying to figure out something.

"How are you doing, today?" I said.

"Fine, thanks. Are you Deepak?" he asked.

"Yes I am. How can I help you?"

"Nice to meet you, Deepak. I'm Tony, the new guy."

"Oh, right. Cindy told me a few minutes ago that you were on lunch," I said. "Nice to meet you too, Tony."

"I've been told that you're the *man*—the top dawg." I laughed, and punched in my ID to start another day.